THE *Empowered* ELA TEACHER

THE *Empowered* ELA TEACHER

CAITLIN MITCHELL &
JESSICA CANNATA

Be The Teacher You Want To Be, Do Great Work, and Thrive.

Dedicated to the wonderful teaching community and team members who make up EB Academics. You commitment to great teaching inspires us.

Some names and identifying details have been changed to protect the privacy of individuals.

Published by EB Academics, San Anselmo, CA
https://ebacademics.com/

GIRL FRIDAY PRODUCTIONS
Edited and designed by Girl Friday Productions
www.girlfridayproductions.com

Design: Rachel Marek
Project management: Katherine Richards
Editorial: Bethany Davis
Image credits: cover © Alexxndr/Shutterstock, prapann/Shutterstock, Igisheva Maria/Shutterstock, and Harper 3D/Shutterstock; p. iv–v, vi, viii, xiv, 14, 31, 36, 40, 76, 105, 106 © Igisheva Maria/Shutterstock; p. 18, 29, 41, 42, 45, 47, 49, 53, 55, 57, 58, 65, 90, 100, 103 © Molly Brett Photography; p. 33 © Elnur/Shutterstock; p. 44 © Independence_Project/Shutterstock; p. 81 © Anna Mente/Shutterstock

ISBN (paperback): 978-0-578-89820-9
ISBN (ebook): 978-0-578-91911-9

Library of Congress Control Number: 2021910173

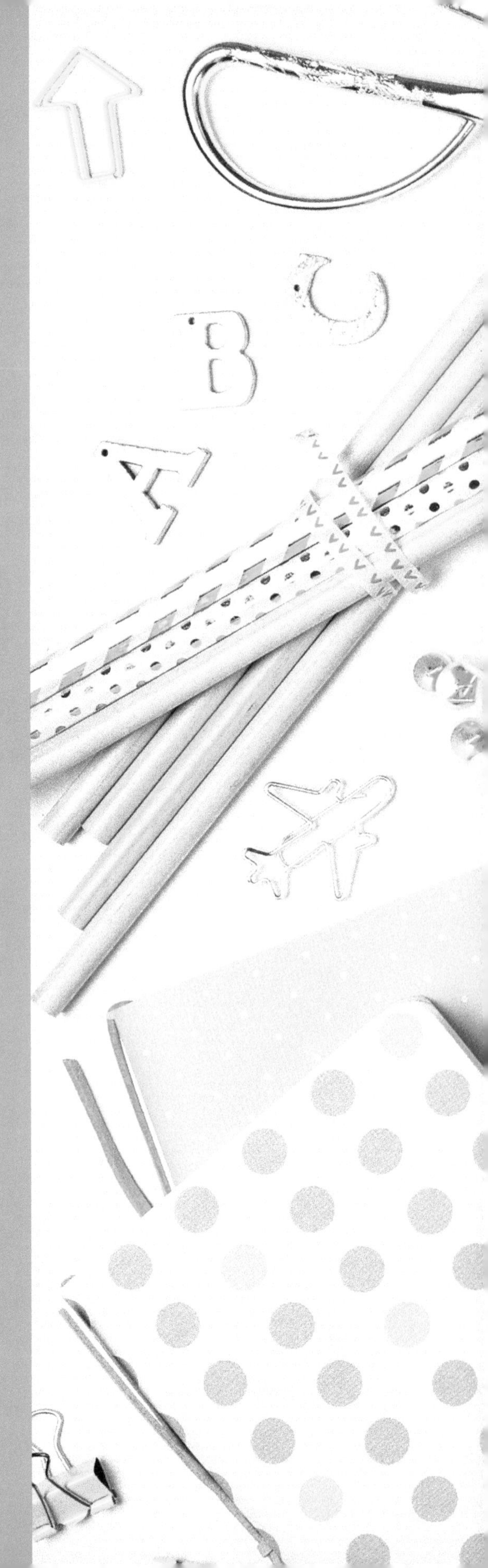

Be. Do. Thrive.

CONTENTS

INTRODUCTION

WHETHER YOU'RE A brand-new middle school English Language Arts teacher, you've been teaching preteens reading and writing for several years, or you're a veteran educator in the field, chances are you've experienced the Sunday Scaries at some point. You know what they are even if you've never heard of them. Here's the deal: Sunday afternoon rolls around, and you let out a sigh and sit down to a cram session of lesson planning, searching online for readymade ELA lessons that never seem to hit the mark, and trying to figure out the puzzle of fitting in all your state standards when you've only got fifty-minute periods each day. (And, if we're being honest, you cast resentful glances at your partner every few minutes as they enjoy a leisurely afternoon binge-watching their latest guilty pleasure on TV.)

These Sunday Scaries are incredibly common in the teaching world; we know all too well how much time teachers spend outside of class each week planning, prepping, grading, decorating bulletin boards, buying classroom supplies, tutoring students, moderating clubs, etc. But what if it didn't have to be this way? What if you could be an empowered educator (and rock star ELA teacher) at your school—heck, even your district—and still walk out the door at 3:00 each day? What if you could deliver engaging and rigorous lessons that didn't take you nights and weekends to plan but still left your students pumped to participate and begging for more? What if you could walk into class each day excited, prepared, and confident to rock your lessons? (Unexpected observation from your administrator? Bring it on!) What if the Sunday Scaries were a thing of the past?

This book is going to walk you through strategies for planning awesome lessons in a fraction of the time you're taking now, using our EB Lesson Planning

Approach. It isn't filled with fluff; instead it's a proven system that ensures engagement and rigor in the classroom and doesn't leave you spending your nights and weekends planning and prepping. It's about helping you *crush* your productivity barriers so you can map out your curriculum and finally find the balance you've been craving between teaching and enjoying the rest of your life.

Is This Book for You?

You are in the right place if you teach middle school ELA (5th–8th grade), if lesson planning is taking up more and more of your free time than you'd like, and if you're ready to put an end to it right now. It's for you if you've been wishing for more engagement (and, frankly, fun) in the classroom while your students master your grade-level ELA standards. It's for you if you're looking for practical tips you can actually use to make your teaching life better and easier. Heck, this is the perfect book if you're required to do some professional development reading. We're not here to bore you!

This book is for you whether you're in year one or year twenty as a middle school ELA teacher. If you're ready to have your best teaching year yet, ready to walk into class each day knowing your students will be more engaged, attentive, and excited to learn while simultaneously achieving or surpassing key grade-level reading and writing skills, then this is the book for you.

Our simple philosophy: Be. Do. Thrive. **BE** the teacher you want to be. **DO** great work. And before you know it, you will **THRIVE**, both in and out of the classroom!

You'll learn the three components of our EB Lesson Planning Approach that will set your students up for success and allow you to become an empowered ELA teacher. This all goes back to our simple philosophy: Be. Do. Thrive. **BE** the teacher you want to be. **DO** great work. And before you know it, you will **THRIVE**, both in and out of the classroom!

Who Are Caitlin and Jessica?

You might be saying to yourself, *All right, this all sounds great, but who's teaching this class? Who are Caitlin and Jessica, and why should I listen to* them? Well, first off, we are former middle school ELA teachers ourselves, and every strategy we talk about in this book we have put into practice. When we started having our own kids, things got real. There was *no way* we could stay late at school or work on the weekends anymore—but we also didn't stop feeling passionate about our jobs and wanting to help our students achieve.

We met teaching across the hall from each other in Los Angeles. Caitlin was the junior high ELA teacher, and Jessica taught 5th grade. We quickly discovered that we had numerous similarities and shared interests (we grew up a half hour away from each other in northern California, went to the same college in LA, have a strange obsession with sourdough bread and Coke . . . we could keep going). But we also share a similar philosophy about teaching. We saw such awesome results with our own students (and with our work-life balance) when we started using the same lesson planning approach that we knew we had to share it with others. So, with growing families of our own and a passion for working with educators around the world to be the empowered ELA teachers at their own schools, we left the classroom in 2019 to focus solely on our business, EB Academics. Since then we've helped thousands of middle school ELA teachers take back their nights and weekends and still deliver rigorous and engaging lessons that get their students mastering the standards.

What You're Going to Learn

What do we think lesson planning should look like? Let's start with what your lesson planning looks like now. It's not the same for every teacher. Some might spend their prep periods and lunch "breaks" planning, some might carve out time to plan each evening, while others may dedicate entire Sunday afternoons to the task.

Some teachers plan everything from scratch. Some spend hundreds and hundreds of dollars on readymade resources. Some create a mix of their own lessons combined with online resources.

However you're lesson planning, it's likely leaving you exhausted before the school week even starts and feeling like you're stuck on a hamster wheel of planning.

So, what sort of lesson planning schedule might work for you? What mix of readymade versus "from scratch" lessons could create the right recipe for your success? What does your daily experience in the classroom indicate about your engagement with the students, and theirs with you?

In **CHAPTER 1**, we begin where you are. We dive deep into the life of the frazzled, overwhelmed teacher—because when you identify where you're starting from, it's easier to see where you can go. Then we can talk about the steps to take to be the teacher you want to be.

THE EMPOWERED ELA TEACHER: KEY COMPONENTS

There are three keys to taking back your nights and weekends while being a dynamic teacher who makes students active participants in their own learning.

1. Engaging Lessons
2. A Commitment to Rigor
3. Effective Lesson Planning

In **CHAPTER 2**, we'll give you an overview of the three key components to help you take back your nights and weekends and still deliver lessons that engage and enrich your students. (Keep in mind, when we say "engage," we don't mean "entertain." Engaged students are actively involved and participating in their learning.)

But it's not enough just to know what these components are. You have to know exactly what to do when you sit down to lesson plan if you want to do great work and see results. So in **CHAPTERS 3 AND 4**, we're sharing proven, rigorous, and engaging activities that will not only get your students mastering the standards, but will also help you feel excited, confident, and prepared to teach each day. We're literally providing you with activity templates that you can immediately use in your classroom to amplify student excitement and start meeting (and exceeding) your grade-level ELA standards.

In **CHAPTER 5**, we'll break down the EB Lesson Planning Approach. You'll learn how to batch plan your lessons, so you don't have to spend each Sunday afternoon stressing about the week ahead. Our EB Teachers say time and again that this is a game-changing strategy that has completely transformed how they lesson plan. (Seriously, you're going to say to yourself, *Why didn't I learn this in any of my teaching classes?*)

CHAPTER 6 is all about stepping into your role as an empowered ELA teacher, the rock star teacher at your school. We'll cover practical tips for maintaining what you've learned so that you can say goodbye for good to that frazzled, overwhelmed teacher—you know, the one who would scarf down a Lean Cuisine at lunch just to have an extra few minutes to finish lesson plans for *The House on Mango Street,* the last one to leave the building every day. That's not going to be you. Not any longer. You will be thriving in and out of the classroom.

Now that you know what you're in for, let's do this!

Chapter 1:

THE MINDSET SHIFT

Why Your Mindset Is So Important

Before we dive into anything covering engagement, rigor, and our EB Lesson Planning Approach, we want to explore what we feel is the single most important aspect of being an empowered ELA teacher—and that is your mindset. You can have all the strategies, tactics, and ideas in the world, but so much of being an empowered educator is about *who you are* and *how you're showing up* each day in your classroom, factors that are directly impacted by your mindset.

If you are walking into your classroom feeling anxious, exhausted, overwhelmed, or however you're feeling right now, how are you delivering your lessons and interacting with your students? Are you simply going through the motions, looking at the clock, and thinking about all the other things you need to accomplish after school before you can head home (grading, copying, researching, prepping, etc.)?

I, Caitlin, know from personal experience just how hard it can be to get excited about a lesson or a concept when you're exhausted from staying up all night trying to figure out what you're going to do the next day in class. Or how frustrating it can be to spend an entire Sunday planning, yet still feel completely overwhelmed by the week ahead before it even begins. I know when I felt that way—exhausted and overwhelmed—it was incredibly challenging for me to be the great teacher I wanted to be.

If you can relate to feeling that same way, which might be why you picked up this book in the first place, we want you to imagine what it would be like to feel the opposite of that. What would teaching be like for you if you felt well rested and completely at ease because your lessons were totally done, organized, and ready for you to pull out each day—you just got to teach? How would you feel? How would you *Be*?

It might sound silly, but this can really have an impact on how you're showing up each day in the classroom. When you're tired and overwhelmed, that stress can show when you get frustrated easily or you aren't as engaged in your lessons as you'd like to be.

And while being well rested and feeling at ease will come much more easily to you after you've learned how to use our EB Lesson Planning Approach, a shift in your mindset is incredibly important as well.

We would love for you to answer the following questions honestly, with the hope that you'll start to see how much of an impact overwhelm and exhaustion can have on us teachers, and ultimately on our students.

If you're tired and stressed when you head to school each morning, are you ready to showcase your greatest abilities as a teacher? Are you walking into your classroom ready to really bring that lesson home for your students that day? Or is the overwhelm putting you in a position where you're showing up but just barely getting by?

The teacher who is **TIRED**, who is **FRANTICALLY** searching through lessons online the night before teaching that concept, who is hanging on by a thread, does not have the **CAPACITY** to ensure all of their students are reaching the standards, let alone mastering them.

An educator at the top of their game (the educator you're about to become) is akin to a professional athlete. Think about how a professional athlete shows up to every game. They're well rested, they've eaten well, they've strategized for *that* specific game to play against *that* specific team.

We don't believe that the empowered ELA teacher is any different from a professional athlete in this regard. A teacher who is at the top of their game is operating at a very different level than the teacher who is barely struggling to get by—barely making it through each day.

The teacher who is tired, who is frantically searching through lessons online the night before teaching that concept, who is hanging on by a thread, does not have the capacity to ensure all of their students are reaching the standards, let alone mastering them.

If this teacher is simply operating on a day-to-day basis, are they taking students' individual data, learning styles, and challenges into account when planning to help them master the standards? Are they able to strategically plan in such a way that their students are participating in engaging activities that all work in conjunction to help students hone particular skills?

More than likely, they aren't.

Think about how that directly affects students. Think about how that affects teachers' ability to perform at their highest, most effective capacity.

It paints a pretty astonishing picture, right?

So if you're feeling this way—like you're barely keeping your head above water—this book is going to help you. It's also important to understand that you're not alone, and it's not you or your fault. It's no surprise that countless teachers struggle to find balance with all that's expected of them beyond just teaching a lesson. Every day, teachers go above and beyond to care for their students, to help them succeed, and to take on all the other responsibilities that come with being a teacher. We don't have to tell you that teachers are underpaid and undervalued for the work they do. But you can be a rock star teacher *and* find that balance.

After reading this book and implementing our approach to becoming an empowered ELA teacher, you will walk away with an entirely new, fresh, and energized mindset. You'll start feeling giddy with anticipation to teach your lessons, and you'll wake up each day with a renewed passion for the profession. Your new mindset will be of paramount importance to finding joy in teaching and continuing to love it year after year.

Your new mindset will be of paramount importance to finding **JOY** in teaching and continuing to love it year after year.

The reason we chose to include a chapter on shifting your mindset has a lot to do with the issues we see pop up over and over again for many in the profession. We do quite a bit of research at our company, EB Academics, to try and understand what teachers are experiencing in their middle school ELA classrooms—how they're feeling, why they're feeling that way, what they need to feel supported, etc.

And over the course of our years of research and in working with thousands of teachers across varying demographics, while we've seen a lot of positivity and excitement for teaching, we've also consistently seen the same frustrations come up time and time again.

One area of stress for many teachers is a massive strain on their personal relationships due to all the time they spend working outside of school. (You know how it looks: your partner wants to cook a nice meal together on Sunday night, and you're online, distracted with your lesson planning.)

Some teachers even feel at a complete loss as to how to help their students, who simply aren't mastering the standards or performing at the level the teachers think they should. (Raise your hand if you've ever stared at a standard you need to teach, completely clueless as to how to teach it, and then headed online and spent hours going down the rabbit hole, trying to find a "just-right" lesson for your students.)

For example, consider the Common Core State Standard for ELA, Reading for Informational Text 7.6: "Determine an author's point of view or purpose in a text and analyze how the author distinguishes his or her position from that of others." Does anyone else's anxiety rise just thinking about everything that needs to be covered there? You now need to find an engaging informational text that has a clear point of view for your students to analyze. You also need to come up with guided questions for them or some kind of activity where they can show they understand the point of view. Then you need to find another text on the same engaging topic, but with an entirely different point of view, and have your students compare and contrast the two texts! You're left asking yourself, *Where do I even begin?* And that's when you spend three hours searching online for interesting articles and feeling overwhelmed at covering this *one* standard, let alone getting your students to master it over the course of the year.

In the worst cases, many teachers feel beat down, burnt out, and on the brink of leaving teaching altogether. (It's their love for their students that keeps them showing up day in and day out.)

It's possible that one of these frustrations speaks to you exactly. Our goal is to make sure you don't continue down a path that is not only detrimental to your relationships with your family, friends, and students, but also detrimental to you.

If something doesn't start to change, at some point you may be tempted to quit teaching altogether. I, Caitlin, can relate all too well, because that's exactly what happened to me.

Now, you might be thinking, *You're writing a book about how to become an empowered ELA teacher. How could you have felt burnout yourself?*

I'm here to tell you that it happened—and very, very early on in my teaching career.

I actually quit. Yes, you read that right. I was done, completely over it, and ready to move on to something where I felt my skills, and what I was capable of, were more appreciated and valued.

And when I say I quit, I don't mean that I waited until May or June to leave. I left seven months into the school year. I gave my thirty-days' notice and left in March.

At the time I was in my fourth year of teaching. I found the profession brutal, and I was stoked to be leaving. There were so many factors that played a role in my departure from the classroom—the long commute; the insane hours I spent each weeknight planning; the overcrowding in my classroom (hello, forty-two students, some without desks). But at the end of the day, it boiled down to one thing: I felt disillusioned with education, and I was utterly exhausted by it.

I had all these grandiose ideas about how I could positively impact our educational system and bring exciting, meaningful lessons into my classroom. But I was young (not that that's an excuse), and I didn't have a supportive administration in the least.

And I let those things get the best of me.

But I will tell you right now that five months later, when I was driving to my new job, a high-stakes sales position in Beverly Hills, I realized it was back-to-school time. I was on a side street, trying to skip past the terrible LA traffic, when I stumbled upon a group of students crossing the street on their first day of school—with their brand-new backpacks on and their perfectly combed and brushed hair, ready to see their friends after a summer's reprieve—and I thought, *Holy crap. What have I done?*

I couldn't believe that I had left teaching, and I realized I had made a huge mistake in doing so. I was meant to be a teacher—it was where my passion in life was. I knew I needed to get back in the classroom, but if I were to go back, something needed to change drastically. I couldn't continue to commit all of my time—hours upon hours upon hours, the long commute, my weekends, every waking hour—to being a teacher.

Teaching could no longer be my entire identity. Instead, teaching needed to be just a part of me.

For so many of us, teaching is our world. We care about our students and want their educational experience to be not just positive, but also memorable and impactful. Sometimes that means being the first one at school in the morning, being the last one to leave, working through lunch, and going beyond what the textbook lessons suggest. But doing all of that takes its toll. Maybe you are close to burnout and quitting like I ultimately did.

But there *is* a way to love teaching, to be an empowered educator impacting students' lives every single school day. And you don't have to work yourself to the bone to get it done.

For so many of us, teaching is our world. We care about our students and want their educational experience to be not just **POSITIVE**, but also **MEMORABLE** and **IMPACTFUL**.

I'm living proof that the transformation is possible. You can transform from the overwhelmed, overworked, exhausted teacher to the empowered ELA teacher who is well rested and filled with excitement each and every day you step into your classroom. The possibility is real. It is attainable. And this book—our strategies, our approach to planning—will get you there.

I can't wait for you to experience the same incredible transformation that I did. You will never feel more empowered, more in tune with the teacher you were meant to be—the teacher you always knew you could be, and the teacher you *will* be.

So let's get to it and jump into the mindset piece.

Are You Playing to Win?

As I, Caitlin, just described, I spent my first few years of teaching with this mindset: *I've just gotta make it through today. One step in front of the other.* I was working just to stay alive, to stay in the profession, so I wouldn't want to quit (which of course I did, so that mindset clearly didn't serve me well).

Every Friday, after an hour-long commute, I would get home around 5:30 and sleep on the couch for hours out of utter exhaustion. It got to the point where I was choosing to put on my pajamas before my husband even got home from work, and microwave something and eat on the couch because I didn't have it in me to cook a meal. Forget about hanging out with my friends on a Friday night—I didn't have the energy. And this was all pre-kids! Once my son was born, teaching all day and then coming home to play with him was a whole new kind of tired.

It was brutal and a miserable way to live.

I wanted to "play to win" (show up energized to teach every single day—excited, confident, and prepared to teach my lessons) instead of "playing to not lose" (struggling to plan out my lessons beyond just a day or two). But I didn't know how to do that.

This was the story of my teaching life: Wake up early. Commute to work. Barely survive each day. Drive home feeling defeated and burnt out. Grade papers and plan lessons at home. Wake up and do it all over again.

What was most frustrating about all of it was that I knew I was a *good teacher*; I was just absolutely wrecking myself to be an amazing teacher.

But it didn't have to be that way. You can be a great teacher without burning the candle at both ends to get it done.

That's what I was able to discover for myself when I came back to the classroom after I left for a year. The magic of what happened was that when I returned, I was more conscientious and strategic about how I was planning and teaching, which allowed me to adopt a new mindset—one where I was "playing to win" each day at school.

I knew that if I wanted to continue on this teaching journey and still be happy, still have time for my family, and still be able to hang out with my friends on the weekend—actually have a life and not let being a teacher consume my entire identity—I needed to change.

I realized that in order to be the best version of myself as a teacher, I needed a new mindset where I was playing to win, showing up each and every day to absolutely crush this teaching thing as an empowered educator. With this new mindset, I knew what I was doing. I was prepared. I was confident. I was going to become the teacher I'd always dreamed of being since I was a young girl playing school with my stuffed animals all lined up in my room.

Of course, we want you to be able to adopt this same "playing to win" mindset as well.

What we're about to say might be hard to hear, so we want you to read the following sentences knowing that, like you, we want what's best for you.

You are the creator of your own destiny.

That's so important, we want to repeat it again: You are the creator of your own destiny.

I realized that in order to be the **BEST VERSION** of myself as a teacher, I needed a new mindset where I was **PLAYING TO WIN**.

In light of that fact, we want to ask you some rapid-fire questions to answer honestly:

Are you blaming outside circumstances—the mandated curriculum, lack of time, difficult lesson planning, students who don't do the work, etc.—for why you don't have the results you want? I, Caitlin, certainly was!

Are you complaining about the results you're seeing in your classroom and how much time you're spending on work outside of school hours? Just ask my husband how many times I called him on my drive home, complaining about the two extra hours I had just stayed at school then being stuck in horrible LA traffic.

Are you doing *just* enough to get by and making excuses about why you're not getting things done or why your students aren't performing the way you want them to in class? I definitely gave more busywork in my early years than I'd like to admit.

Are you playing to not lose? Or are you playing to *win*?

Are you committed to becoming an empowered educator even when it feels hard and stressful (which it won't after you implement the EB Lesson Planning Approach—we've got your back!)?

Are you ready, willing, and prepared with an open heart and mind to step into your role of an empowered ELA teacher with a new mindset and a new approach to lesson planning?

Since you're the creator of your own destiny, you have full control to step into a whole new role and mindset of an empowered educator, and you will no longer be teaching from the perspective of "playing to not lose."

You will no longer be doing things like endlessly searching the internet for lessons that don't actually help your students, spending late nights planning for the very next day, bringing home a bag full of textbooks that never get touched, or working all Sunday long. Those were all things that I, Caitlin, used to do in those first few years of teaching when I was playing to not lose. All of the things that ultimately made me quit. Which is *not* what you're about to do.

Now, if anything we just said made you feel uncomfortable or perhaps even mad, good!

Our growth as teachers happens when we experience discomfort. That's when we make changes and start doing even greater work.

When you face your discomfort and start learning what to do and what not to do, you will find you're building your teaching skills, taking action, and expanding your ability to handle challenges. This is how you start playing to win.

Playing to win is about **TAKING ACTION** and investing in strategies that will take you further faster.

Why do you think empowered, well-balanced ELA teachers are so few and far between?

Because most people do not want to wade into the discomfort.

Most people hate uncertainty and aren't willing to face their fears and get out of their comfort zone. So they stay the same and then wonder why they don't get different results, the ones they want.

Playing to win is about taking action and investing in strategies that will take you further faster. This book did not come into your hands by chance. Something in life led you to this very moment, to read this very sentence.

By simply being *here*, you are investing your time in reading it to help you take action and move further into your role of empowered ELA teacher much faster.

So, are you ready to adopt a new mindset where you always play to win? Where you're confident in the lessons you're creating and delivering? Where there's balance between your personal life and your teaching life? Where you feel prepared not just for tomorrow's lesson and the next day's, but even next month's? Where you begin each day excited to teach—in fact, saying, *Bring it on!* to those teacher observations because you know you're going to rock that lesson?

Are You Really Committed to This?

We've discussed some of the detrimental effects that can take hold in your life when you allow "overwhelm" to get the best of you. You don't want to be the overwhelmed, exhausted teacher that we discussed at the beginning of this chapter. You don't want strained relationships with family members because lesson planning and teaching are taking over time with your loved ones. You don't want to see your students struggling in your classroom. You don't want to up and quit one day, never to look back.

So we know what you don't want.

But what do you really, really want? (Did anyone else just get transported back to the '90s and start singing "Wannabe"? Maybe that's just us.) Do you really want to be an empowered ELA teacher—the educator at your school that everyone else at your school looks at, wondering, *What the heck are you doing to get your students to love your class so much? And how the heck are you doing it so effortlessly?*

If you are really committed to stepping into this role of empowered educator, then we have to ask: Are you willing to put in the time and effort to make that happen? And yes, it will require time and effort.

Because *right now* is the time for you to decide. Who and how do you want to *be* as a teacher?

Saying what you want is one thing, but actually making it happen is another. We're going to give you our entire lesson planning approach in this book—all our suggestions, our frameworks, everything—but it's 100 percent up to *you* to commit to implementing what we share.

Anyone can pick up this book and read it, but it's up to *you* to be the teacher with the drive and tenacity to put everything into practice and create the life you want for yourself. You have to truly want this.

Looking back on a specific experience that I, Caitlin, had when I was a teenager, I can see that I fell into that realm of *saying* I wanted something to happen, but not going beyond that.

I remember playing on my high school varsity basketball team and constantly saying that I wanted to be the starting point guard my senior year. I worked hard for three years to make that a reality, but then my senior year, a talented freshman point guard joined our team, and I knew I was going to be riding the bench unless I made something happen for myself.

And you know what? I didn't make anything happen for myself. I kept saying over and over again how much I wanted that starting position, but I did nothing beyond showing up and working hard in practice to make it happen.

Had I truly wanted that starting position, I would have given every ounce of me to make it happen. During practice, I would have asked my coach what skills I could be working on to improve my jump shot or my ability to "see the court." I needed to trust him and put into action his recommendations for me. But I didn't.

Instead, the only reason I ended up getting to start my senior year was because the talented freshman injured her knee during a preseason game, and I was called in to play.

I would have done so much more if I had really wanted that starting position, and I would have appreciated it so much more if I had earned it.

But when I look back now at what I didn't do, I realize that I didn't want that spot as badly as the freshman who came in and took it. In fact, that freshman point guard went on to play Division 1 college basketball and become a college basketball coach. My basketball career ended the moment I graduated high school.

Clearly there was a difference between the talented freshman and me, and the outcome of our basketball careers was a direct reflection of what was important to us.

It's the same with teaching. It's not enough to want work-free weekends and rock star lessons. You have to really *want* it to happen, with the fortitude and desire within you to do whatever it takes to make that your reality.

You say you want to be the best middle school ELA teacher you can be, right? That's why you picked up this book and are reading it right now.

> This is so much bigger than what you **SAY** you want to do.

You say you want to stop sacrificing your nights and weekends and your time with family and friends.

You say you want to get your students to love learning—to be engaged in school and mastering those challenging standards.

Saying it is great.

But now it's time to actually make that commitment to yourself. And we know you can do it!

This is so much bigger than what you say you want to do. Remember, this is all about that mindset piece—how *who you are* affects your ability to become an empowered educator. So now you need to move out of the state of saying you want something and into a state of what we like to call "perpetual doing."

This means that from here on out, you will start implementing the strategies in this book. You're not going to read it one June and then forget everything you read by the time school starts up again in August. Instead you'll read the book in June and then consistently review the ideas and apply them throughout the school year—a state of perpetual doing.

Right now, in this moment, you are promising to make one of the most important shifts you can make as a teacher.

You are committing 100 percent to shifting *away* from a state of wanting and shifting *into* a state of doing. You are going to stop talking about what you do or don't want. You will now start doing what you do want.

You are going to become the creator of your own reality—the reality of an empowered ELA teacher.

Chapter 2:

THE EMPOWERED ELA TEACHER

THREE PRINCIPLES OF THE EMPOWERED ELA TEACHER

1. **ENGAGEMENT:** think games and escape rooms.
2. **RIGOR:** think evidence trackers and literary analysis responses.
3. **LESSON PLANNING FRAMEWORK:** think a template that saves your sanity when lesson planning.

THE MAGIC OF stepping into your role of Empowered ELA Teacher lies in adopting three main principles—engagement, rigor, and a lesson planning framework.

Adopting these principles will move you from the teacher you are into actively becoming the one you want to be. You just need to *Do* the work. Seems pretty darn simple, right?

That's because it is.

But so often these essential principles get overlooked, or one gets more emphasis than another, or we were never taught to incorporate it into our teaching in the first place.

Well, that will no longer be the case for you once you finish working through this book and begin implementing these principles into your teaching practice.

It's important to note that all three of these principles have to work in conjunction with each other. You can't simply have engagement without rigor and a planning framework, or even a planning framework and engagement without rigor. They *all* hold equal importance and value, and they will all work together to help you achieve your goal of being the best educator possible.

Let's talk first about engagement. If you're missing the engagement aspect, your lessons might be challenging, appropriate, and well planned, but your students will hate showing up and won't ever get excited by the material, much less put their best effort into their work. You want your students to *love* school and walk out of class talking to their friends about the lesson. They won't be doing that if they're simply trudging through worksheets.

On the flip side, if your lessons lack rigor (which is based largely in the standards) and your students are just having fun, then there is little chance of ever meeting or exceeding the standards. By "rigor," we don't only mean how challenging the lessons are; we mean how they are structured, and if they cover all the bases that need to be covered as far as standards are concerned. This leads to the question: Why are you even teaching what you're teaching, anyhow? Sure, it's great to have everything planned and your students excited to come to class each day, but if they're not mastering the standards and meeting the requirements, what are you doing? How are you showing and measuring their growth over time?

Finally, if you're missing the planning aspect, you might have absolutely stellar lessons that get your students mastering the standards, loving school, and excited to show up to class—but what happens to you? You're going to end up utterly burnt out, exhausted, and on the brink of quitting. It happened to me (Caitlin). I do not want that same experience for you.

So. All three principles work with and complement each other. They *must* all be woven together.

What's cool about incorporating these three main principles into your teaching is what happens as a result.

You set out with a specific intention—to be a better teacher—but that's not the only outcome. Over time, you'll start to notice a multitude of astonishing outcomes that weren't even on your mind when you set out on this quest.

Jessica and I saw ridiculously positive results at a faculty meeting in 2013, where the focus was on reviewing and analyzing the data from our students' recent standardized tests. As we were looking through the scores across all grade levels, our principal noticed something remarkable about the ELA scores in 5th, 7th, and 8th grade (our grade levels): student test scores had soared that year.

Now, we knew what we were doing in our classrooms was helping our students master the ELA standards and become critical readers and writers, but to see the data corroborate all of our subjective observations was something else.

You set out with a specific **INTENTION**—to be a better teacher—but that's not the only **OUTCOME**.

That year marked a change in the way that we chose to approach ELA as a whole in our middle school. Engagement, rigor, and planning were at the core of everything we did.

Not only did we witness our students performing at very high levels, we also saw how invested they were in their learning and an increased excitement in participation each day. More and more students were naturally asking questions and starting conversations about the literature we were studying.

For example, one of my (Caitlin's) favorite activities was a prereading exercise with controversial questions to lead us into *The Tragedy of Romeo and Juliet*. I'd post questions around the classroom—"What age is too young to marry?"

"Can loyalty ever go too far?" "Can love happen at first sight?"—questions that would get students' interest piqued and opinions riled up before we dove into the material.

I vividly remember my most recent 8th grade class getting heated about each of these questions—students sitting around the school yard at recess, saying to each other, "How old do you think Romeo and Juliet were when they got married?" "Do you think loyalty had something to do with them dying?"

So good! They were having beyond-the-classroom discussions about *Romeo and Juliet* before they had even started reading it.

When I, Jessica, was reading one of my all-time favorite novels, *The Westing Game*, with my 5th graders, the investment and excitement from my students was palpable. They begged to stay inside at recess and keep reading. They debated and discussed different theories while waiting in line for morning assembly. They even convinced their parents to read the book! Why? Because it was *fun*. We deciphered clues to solve the mystery, created detective groups to search for evidence, and created social media profiles for the characters.

After reading chapter 22, one of my students spontaneously jumped up and down and screamed out in excitement when she discovered what the clues revealed. The rest of the class rushed to the board where our clues were written, so she could show them what she'd figured out. It made my teacher heart happy seeing the level of excitement about a book we were reading.

Another ripple effect that you'll start to see when you apply the three principles is the change that occurs in you. You will inherently become more engaged as a teacher.

You see, there's a basic law of reciprocity that says we get out of something what we put into it. If you're putting engagement front and center in your mind as one of your guiding principles as a teacher, what are you going to get out of your lessons and your interactions with your class?

You'll be engaged in your own classroom and lessons!

You'll be excited to show up and teach, every single day!

What a difference it makes when you wake up each day eager to go to school. You're pumped because you've got an incredible lesson up your sleeve that you know your students are going to love.

When you wake up with that mindset, when you show up to work in that mindset with a big grin on your face, stoked to be at school, what becomes possible for you? What becomes possible for your students?

In addition to that, when you make rigor a priority in your lessons, you push your students further. You're constantly thinking of ways to make certain lessons more challenging, to allow your students to think outside the box, to show you what they're capable of and rise to the occasion.

WHAT IS A SOCRATIC SEMINAR?

A Socratic seminar is a group-based discussion using open-ended questions that invite critical thinking. If you haven't done one yet, definitely add it to your must-try activities list! Don't worry, we've got you covered. In the appendix we'll provide you with some Socratic seminar templates to get started.

Caitlin speaking here. The night before I was going to try my very first Socratic seminar with my new 8th grade class, I couldn't sleep. Not just because my principal was going to be there as part of my formal observations, but because I'd *really* put forth a challenge for my students, and I couldn't wait to see the result.

Did it run the risk of absolute failure and falling completely on its face? Sure. But we'll never know what our students are truly capable of unless we give them the opportunity to show us. So I thought, *Why the heck not?* Since this was the beginning of the year, I really wanted to push them. I thought, *Let's see how far they can go to meet me with this lesson. Let's make it as difficult as possible.*

I based our Socratic seminar around an excerpt from Ralph Waldo Emerson's essay "Self-Reliance." Yes, I had my 8th graders participate in their first seminar using a high-school-level text that was challenging to decipher in and of itself, let alone hold a critical and thoughtful discussion around.

We'll never know what our students are truly **CAPABLE** of unless we give them the opportunity to **SHOW US**.

I woke up early that Thursday morning with all of the jitters I would normally have on the first day of school. *How is this going to go? Are my students going to just sit there silently with awkward looks on their faces? Is that one student going to be distracted, looking out the window and not participating in the lesson? Will my principal think,* Wait a minute? I came here to observe Caitlin. How come she's just sitting there silently in the corner of the room?

I stepped into my classroom at 7:30 a.m. and quickly arranged the desks into an inner circle with an outer circle, a hot seat clearly labeled, and my teacher chair firmly planted off to the side, so as not to interfere with or lead the discussion.

This was to be all on my students.

As my 8th graders poured into the classroom and got their notes and annotated essays out, I saw my principal walk in and park himself at my desk with his clipboard, ready to take notes and make observations about this lesson.

My jitters turned into excitement about what was to unfold, and that had me grinning from ear to ear. I couldn't help but be filled with immense pride in my students—even if the lesson turned out to be a dud. We were at least going to give this a shot.

Ten or fifteen minutes into the discussion, I glanced over at my principal, whose eyes were filled with awe. I looked around intently at my students. They were wrapped up in a discussion of self-identity and nonconformity. I started to cry (for real). I was so proud. They were knocking it out of the park in every way possible.

Three years into my career teaching both middle school and high school English, I was confident in my ability to deliver engaging and rigorous lessons. But it was still taking me hours and hours every weekend to create them. What I was missing was a lesson planning framework that freed up my nights and weekends.

Then in 2013, my fourth year of teaching, I finally started to implement, rather unintentionally, a specific approach to planning. This was the year that Jessica and I started teaching together (in fact, it's the *only* year we taught together—if you can believe that), and I vividly remember Jessica leaving school every day by 3:00 p.m.

I couldn't help but think, *What on* earth *is she doing? How is she able to leave so early?*

At this point in my career, I was already familiar with creating a year-long scope and sequence (which we'll go into detail about later, in our lesson planning chapter), so I had my entire school year planned out. But I still wasn't quite in a position where I was leaving school at 3:00 every day, like Jessica was.

I started getting jealous. I wanted to be doing that too.

I wanted to close my classroom doors and bring only my purse home instead of a massive teacher bag filled with books, lesson plans, and work that needed grading.

I became determined to figure out a way to also leave at 3:00 p.m. And no way was this going to be like my experience wanting to be the starting point guard in high school. I didn't just *want* to leave at 3:00, I was going to do everything I could to make it happen.

I have to be honest for a moment. As great as it would be for the narrative of this book for me to have gone to Jessica and asked for help, that isn't what happened. I was a little bit afraid to ask Jessica for any of her time, because she had a newborn at home. She spent her lunches and breaks racing home to feed her baby, Jameson—Can anyone else relate? Talk about having *no* time to plan, if you have a baby and are still teaching!—and would leave right after school to get back to him.

Thankfully, the way I lesson planned was already quite similar to what Jessica was doing at that point. (Scope and sequence, engaging and rigorous lessons—check.)

But what was missing in how I lesson planned was a simple but incredibly important component of the EB Lesson Planning Approach: batch planning. Turns out, batch planning was Jessica's secret to leaving at 3:00 p.m.! So that's when I started batch planning too.

In chapter 6, we're going to share exactly what we do, step by step, so that you can also batch plan rigorous and engaging lessons and get out the door by 3:00 p.m.

So, let's review. An Empowered ELA Teacher incorporates engagement, rigor, and a lesson planning framework so that they can feel excited, confident, and prepared to teach each day without sacrificing their nights and weekends.

Let's dive in to that first component, all about engagement.

Chapter 3:

THE POWER OF ENGAGING LESSONS

I, JESSICA, KNEW my sophomore Spanish class was going to be fun the minute I walked into the room. It didn't hurt that Connor, my high school crush, was in the class too. But mostly it was the fact that Ms. Neilan was my teacher. I knew I was lucky to have her; she was only twenty-three years old and full of energy. She loved playing games and having us do skits to help us learn the material. This was a stark contrast from my freshman Spanish class with Señora Taravel, who had us conjugate lists of verbs and fill in worksheets each day. Instead, Ms. Neilan had us play Scattergories with our vocabulary words, do weekly skits to practice conversational Spanish, and ultimately make our own movies for the annual Academy Awards ceremony she put on at the end of the year.

I remember one particular class, when we were in the middle of a unit about family members and learning the Spanish words for husband, wife, etc., and Ms. Neilan had us doing skits acting out a marriage proposal. My crush, Connor, was supposed to ask his partner to marry him, she would answer the proposal, and then the rest of the class was supposed to say, *"Felicidades!"*

> I knew what kind of teacher I wanted to be: one who made lessons **SO ENGAGING** and fun that students got lost in their learning.

Well, right before Connor and his partner got up for their turn in front of the class, Ms. Neilan came over to me and whispered in my ear that I should interrupt them in the middle of their skit and pretend that I was secretly in love with Connor and didn't want him to go through with the proposal. I was mortified. I had butterflies in my stomach, the whole nine yards. What were my classmates (and Connor!) going to think? They had no idea Ms. Neilan had asked me to do this.

I worked up the courage and interrupted their skit, saying in my very limited Spanish something along the lines of "No, I love you. Please marry me." I was so nervous that I honestly don't remember the rest of the skit or what anyone said. But I do remember all of us laughing when it was finally over and Ms. Neilan explained that she had asked me to jump in.

My point is that it was fun and silly and we were all entertained. (It did not, however, lead to a date with Connor. Oh well!)

The Spanish material Ms. Neilan covered was rigorous, but it stuck with me because she made it so much fun. I looked forward to sixth-period Spanish each day, and the fifty minutes flew by because I was completely engaged in whatever activity Ms. Neilan had in store for us.

Her teaching style impacted me as a fifteen-year-old. Her engaging lessons encouraged me to continue learning Spanish long after it was a requirement. They also had an impact on me as a future educator. I already knew I wanted to be a teacher, and at fifteen, after having been in Ms. Neilan's class for just a few weeks, I knew what kind of teacher I wanted to be: one who made lessons so engaging and fun that students got lost in their learning. You better believe I took note of the games and activities we did and stored them away in the back of my mind to use later with my own students.

Wherever Ms. Neilan is today, I would love for her to know what an impact she had on me later, when I was a teacher in my own classroom, and even now that I'm a curriculum developer, spending my days creating engaging lessons.

Engaging lessons are incredibly powerful and produce countless unexpected ripple effects. They also serve as steady reminders that learning can be fun. And when students make the connection that learning isn't just rote memorization, but an enjoyable opportunity to explore and be challenged, then they too will want to continue learning long after the last bell rings.

This chapter is all about diving deep into the power of engaging lessons. But before we reflect on the ripple effects of bringing engagement into the classroom, there are a few questions we need to address. What does an engaging lesson look like? How can we make sure to include engagement in our lessons? It's not a one-size-fits all situation: what one student finds enjoyable, another might find terrifying. We're going to explore these topics and make a case for why engagement is one of the main components of a great lesson, and how to apply engagement in the best way, to reach as many students as possible.

Engaging lessons are incredibly powerful and produce countless **UNEXPECTED** ripple effects. They also serve as steady reminders that learning can be **FUN**.

And here's what we're most excited about: we'll be sharing a whole bunch of engaging lesson ideas you can use with your own students, along with pictures and step-by-step instructions for how to implement them in your classroom. Think of this like a sneak peek into another teacher's classroom, where you get to steal all the ideas you like and start using them immediately.

But before we get to all those goodies, let's go deeper in exploring why incorporating engagement into your lessons is so critical.

Why Engagement Is Critical

Jessica here. My husband and I recently introduced our two oldest sons to *Ferris Bueller's Day Off*, and now they are constantly saying, "Bueller? Bueller?" to each other in deadpan voices. Can't you just hear the monotone voice of Ferris's teacher (Ben Stein) taking attendance? I cringe at the thought of what his lessons might have been like—although I had a professor just like that in college. It was a freshman-level history class, and you know how it is when you're a freshman; you get the last pick of classes. So there I was, meeting my history requirement in an 8:00 a.m. class three mornings a week. Now, I'm a morning person, but this class was so incredibly dull that I distinctly remember nodding off a time or two that fall semester. The professor lectured the entire fifty minutes each Monday, Wednesday, and Friday, rattling off dates and details in rapid-fire succession. Clearly the man knew his World War I history, but he delivered it in the driest, dullest way imaginable—no stories, no projects, no group work, nothing. My entire grade was based on a comprehensive research paper, a midterm, and a final.

> When we teachers engage our students, we get their **BUY-IN** and they become **INVESTED** in their learning. And having student buy-in makes everything about the lesson better.

That freshman history class was the lowest grade I ever got in college, and I 100 percent believe that my poor grade reflected how disengaged I was in the lessons. And this may seem off topic, but I think it reinforces my point. Ten years later, my boyfriend (now my husband) and I were reminiscing about college classes. We attended the same school but didn't meet until a month after graduation. As I was describing this horrible history class to him, he started asking questions like, "Was that class in University Hall?" (Yes!) "Was the professor a tall man with a crew cut?" (Yes!) "Was it the History of World War I?" (Yes!) It turns out my future husband was in that early-morning class with me but transferred into a different class after two weeks. He said to me, "Why did you stay in that class? It was awful. I was bored out of my mind!" This, from my history-loving husband. Funny to think how our paths might have crossed much sooner. (He says it's a good thing we didn't date in college: I probably wouldn't have liked his fraternity-boy lifestyle!) But now I really am getting off topic. The point is that this ridiculously boring history class made a negative impact on both of us.

So why do we advocate for engagement in the classroom and consider it a key aspect of becoming an empowered ELA teacher? After all, teachers aren't cruise directors. We're not expected to entertain our students each day with scheduled social activities. But remember, there is a difference between *entertaining* students (providing them with amusement and enjoyment) and *engaging* students (providing them with opportunities that allow them to give their best each day because they are motivated and committed to the lesson's goal and outcome).

When students are engaged in their learning, they are **MOTIVATED** to do well and thus take pride in their work.

When we teachers engage our students, we get their buy-in and they become invested in their learning. And having student buy-in makes everything about the lesson better. No groans of protest when we ask students to do something; rather, when they are engaged, they take initiative and ask to keep working or want to know what they can do to solve the problem. (Not to mention the fact that behavior issues all but disappear!) When students buy in to the lessons, they build relationships with one another and with us. Everyone is on the same team, working collaboratively toward common goals.

Engaging lessons also foster increased participation and discussion; problem solving and strategizing occur naturally as students communicate more with one another. They are not simply passively receiving information (as I did in my History of WWI class). They are analyzing, synthesizing, and applying information.

When students are engaged in their learning, they are motivated to do well and thus take pride in their work. And when they are doing their best and feeling good about their work, their confidence increases. They connect to the content because they have a vested interest in it. And when interest and engagement are present, meaningful and authentic learning can occur.

ENGAGEMENT BUILDS EXCITEMENT ABOUT LEARNING

While working on the Edgar Allan Poe Escape Room from "The Cask of Amontillado" unit, I had one student who really came out of his shell during this specific activity. I could see the excitement on his face and could hear it in his voice as he continued to work on each task with his group. It turns out that his group was the winning group and escaped first. At the end of the class this student, and others, came up to me and said, "Mrs. Cassidy, class was so much fun today! I hope we do more activities like that in the future." *—Ashli Cassidy*

We can all agree that student buy-in, increased participation, and helping students connect with the content are what we all strive to accomplish in our middle school ELA classrooms. But how do we do it? What does it actually look like to achieve these results? Let's break down each component in further detail and share some ideas for nailing down engaging lessons.

Creating Student Buy-In

Of course, we want our students to look forward to coming to our class, to have so much fun that they don't even realize they're learning, and to buy in to the material. And a huge part of that comes down to how we deliver the content to our students. Do we simply lecture and provide worksheets, scrambling to fit all our content into a fifty-minute period? Or do we come up with games and activities that are fun for everyone but don't take hours and hours of planning?

We'll be honest: it can be intimidating to come up with interesting and creative ways to deliver content—especially when some of the grade-level Common Core State Standards for ELA are notoriously dull! (We're looking at you, Reading Informational Text 7.2: "Determine two or more central ideas in a(n) [informational] text and analyze their development. . . .")

But remember, a little trepidation about the standards isn't going to stop us from coming up with engaging lessons. Nope, we're going to lean into the uncertainty and take small, actionable steps, because we're ready to embrace what's on the other side: an empowered educator whose students are highly engaged in learning and mastering the standards!

So if we want to get student buy-in, we need to be the teachers who are always on the lookout for a fun, unique angle that can be used to deliver content.

Generating Engaging Ideas

The absolute very first step for bringing engagement into your classroom is to start generating a go-to list of inspiring ideas that you can apply to your ELA lessons. It helps to have a notebook to keep track of any inspiring ideas you come across. Nothing is off limits; it doesn't matter how outlandish the idea is. No one says you actually have to use it, but having the idea written down may inspire other ideas. That's it. You're going to start a list of ideas and commit to jotting them down in a central spot.

I, Jessica, keep an ongoing list of inspiring ideas. Below are just a few of them, including how they popped into my head:

- Snowball Fight: My sons were having a "snowball" fight with wadded-up pieces of paper.
- *The Amazing Race*: A reality show with this title popped up as a recommendation on my Prime Video list.
- *Escape from Alcatraz*: I was reading *Al Capone Does My Shirts* to my sons at bedtime.
- Pretty Paint Chips: We were remodeling our home.
- Spoons: The card game, not the utensil!
- Gingerbread House for Sale: This descriptive writing activity came from looking at one of my mom's real estate flyers on our kitchen counter.

THE POWER OF A SIMPLE IDEA

This year in December I did the "Gingerbread House for Sale" unit, and it was amazing. I started by turning the outside of my room into a Gingerbread House with a FOR SALE sign, to add excitement. This activity pulled the absolute best out of my students. Their descriptive writing hit a level far beyond my expectations (and I have very high expectations). I had to find a way to showcase their work, so we hung our flyers in the hallway and held an open house, in which we invited the other teachers, support staff, and even administration to come "purchase the gingerbread house of their dreams." Once a home was purchased I hung a SOLD sign on it for all to see. It was a huge hit, because the students got to see the impact of their writing. They kept coming to my hallway to see if their house had SOLD! *—Shanda Burnett*

This list of ideas is constantly changing and evolving, but every so often I take a look at it to see if something on it sparks an idea for a lesson that I think will get student buy-in. I mean, what student wouldn't love a snowball fight in the classroom?

Again, it doesn't matter if you actually use every idea on the list. The purpose is to think outside the box and get the creative juices flowing. So often in the classroom, we teach a lesson simply because that's the way we've always done it or that's the way it's outlined in our teacher's manual. But what if we stumble across a new and brilliant way to deliver an activity? One that makes us giddy with excitement to teach that day, because we know our students are going to *love* it? We shouldn't deprive ourselves or our students of all that fun just because it's easier to teach a lesson the same way we know and are comfortable with.

So now it's your turn. Start generating a list of inspiring ideas that could potentially lead to a lesson in your classroom. Don't censor yourself. No idea is a bad idea. And if you're anything like us and it helps to write your list on a pretty piece of stationery, then by all means do it! Anything that helps you actually do the work.

Do.

My Inspiring Ideas

1.

2.

3.

4.

5.

6.

And because life is busy and crazy and messy sometimes, it's important to make this a habit. Jot down an idea every morning right after you brush your teeth, or after yoga class every Tuesday and Thursday evening, or whatever works for you. You simply want to be adding fresh ideas each week, and if you do it consistently, you are much more likely to actually use some of these ideas for future lessons.

This should be no surprise, but if you want to see change, you have to take action. If you want to deliver fun and engaging ELA lessons that have you excited to teach each day, it's all about taking little steps to reach that goal.

Some of you are probably reading this and thinking, *I'll just remember my ideas. I don't need to write them down.* We know you have great intentions, but there's a commitment that comes with putting something down in writing. Everyone reading this has access to the same ideas and information, yet it's the teachers who actually do the work (and honestly, just jotting down an inspirational idea each day isn't that hard!) who will see the results.

Those who write down their ideas will be more likely to transform them into fun, engaging lessons. They will see the joy on students' faces when they participate in something special. And little by little the lessons will add up, until one day these teachers will realize that they are no longer burnt out, but inspired to try new ideas and approaches to the material they know so well.

So stop reading right now and jot down at least five fun memories, experiences, or ideas. If you're having trouble getting started, use these prompts:

- Where would you love to travel if you could go anywhere in the world?
- What's the best Halloween costume you ever wore?
- What's the most memorable field trip you took in elementary school?
- What's the title of a book you're currently reading?
- What's your go-to order from a fast-food restaurant? (Ours would hands down be a veggie burrito from Chipotle with a side of guacamole!)

Do.

Idea #1

Idea #4

Idea #2

Idea #5

Idea #3

Turning Your List of Inspiring Ideas into Actual Lessons

Are you ready to see an example in action of how I, Jessica, took an idea from my inspiration list and turned it into a full-blown lesson? I'll break it down in detail here.

I'm constantly adding games that my own three children play to my list of inspiring ideas. My sons are really into card games right now. (I swear my five-year-old, Davy, is a card shark—he regularly skunks my husband and me in Gin Rummy.) Both my sons really like the card game Spoons. In that game, cards are quickly passed around until a player gets four of a kind. That player takes a spoon from the center, and then everyone else must quickly take one too. The last player without a spoon is out. We had so much fun playing as a family one night (of course, Davy won) that I knew I had to add Spoons to my list of inspiring ideas.

Fast-forward to a few weeks later, when I was planning a unit on narrative writing. I knew that I wanted my students to include a heavy dose of figurative language in their narratives, and that we'd need to review all the different types of figurative language before they began writing.

Of course, I could have simply provided students with a list of figurative-language devices and their definitions, but I wanted to include a more memorable activity to help the examples stick.

So I skimmed my trusty list of inspiring ideas to see if something could tie into figurative language. When I saw Spoons, I knew I'd found a perfect opportunity. Using card stock which I then laminated—what teacher doesn't love an excuse to laminate something?—I made a deck of cards, each with one of the following types of figurative language typed on one side: simile, metaphor, personification, alliteration, assonance, onomatopoeia, hyperbole, oxymoron, and allusion. Then I came up with three cards that could potentially match each type of figurative language. For *simile*, for example, the cards looked like this:

1. Simile
2. "She tried to get rid of the kitten which had scrambled up her back and stuck like a burr just out of reach." —*Little Women*, Louisa May Alcott
3. When she smiles, her eyes are like diamonds.
4. Definition: a comparison using *like* or *as*.

OLD McDONALD

Side note: If you or your students struggle to spell *onomatopoeia*, try spelling it to the tune of "Old McDonald Had a Farm": O-N-O-M-A-T-O-P-O-E-I-A. I always taught my students this trick, and it stuck—they could spell it no problem! (You just sang it to yourself, didn't you?)

Once I created all my cards, I simply made copies of the cards and then organized my students into groups of four or five. Each group sat in a small circle with plastic spoons in the center (one fewer spoon than there were players in the group). The cards were shuffled, and each student was dealt four cards. The remaining cards formed a stack in the middle. Player 1 took a card from the stack, placed it in their hand, then quickly got rid of a card by passing it facedown to the next student in the circle (clockwise). Just like in a regular game of Spoons, the goal was to get four of a kind, except in this case students needed four cards representing the same type of figurative language (the actual type of figurative language, the definition, and/or an example). Once a player took a spoon from the middle, the rest of the players could also grab a spoon, even if they did not have four cards representing a particular type of figurative language. The player who grabbed the first spoon would show their cards to the group so they all could agree that the hand was a correct figurative-language match.

Students loved playing this game, and because it was **HANDS-ON** and interactive, it helped them **RETAIN** the information better and actually use figurative language in their narratives.

Students loved playing this game, and because it was hands-on and interactive, it helped them retain the information better and actually use figurative language in their narratives.

If you're reading this and thinking, *This might be fun, but it sounds like a lot of work for just one game,* consider that once you create it (and laminate it!), you can use this activity for years to come. It's also a great activity for early finishers or to have on hand when a last-minute sub is needed. What a wonderful opportunity to use this game multiple times throughout the year, to spiral figurative-language concepts into your curriculum.

After reading this, can you think of other ELA concepts that can be used to play Spoons? How about a grammar review (for a super-challenging ga you could cover the different sentence types: simple, compound, complex, and compound-complex) or an introduction to literary elements?

Take a few minutes to jot down some ideas below for how you could tie Spoons into your curriculum.

P.S.: Later in this chapter, we'll be sharing other game ideas you can implement in your classroom, along with student directions already completed for you, so you can use these games with your students.

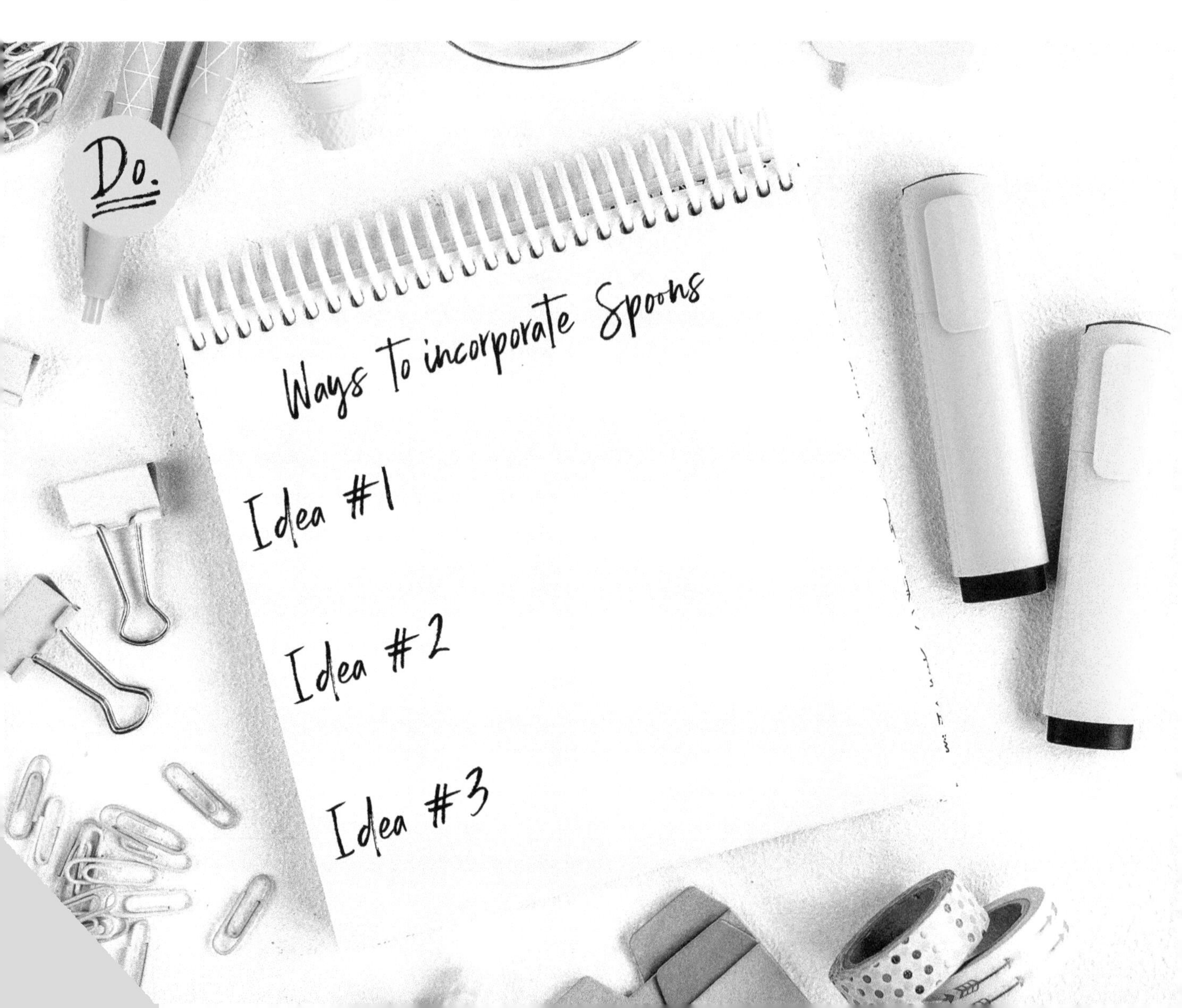

Increasing Student Participation

Take a minute and think about the last professional development session you were required to attend. I, Jessica, have been to my fair share of these throughout the course of my teaching career—easily more than a hundred different sessions. In the district where I worked most recently, they used to be the fourth Monday of every month. And for the life of me, I cannot tell you the specifics of any single one of these sessions. Sure, they covered the usual topics: differentiation, vocabulary instruction, the latest writing method our district wanted us to adopt. But even if pressed, I could not tell you any major takeaways. Why? I'm sure that like the majority of the PD sessions you've been to, the ones I attended were dull and monotonous. We received a packet of handouts, followed along with a PowerPoint, and met in grade-level groups to discuss strategy (of course, this just turned into teachers venting and gossiping).

And although I'm sure all these presenters put a lot of effort into their presentations, they completely missed the mark on including any form of engagement. So when it came time to participate, the audience of teachers usually tried to keep a low profile and slyly returned to the pile of essays they were grading, hoping to avoid detection. Let's face it, more often than not, we believed we could have been using this time better than sitting in an outdated auditorium, listening to the presenter drone on about the latest trend in education.

Had there just been some effort to engage us in the topic, our attention would have shifted from the essays we'd brought along to the topic being presented.

The same dynamic applies to our students. When they are engaged in their learning, their participation increases. And this increase in participation can occur with either teacher-directed learning (lectures) or student-led learning (group projects). It's important to note that participation doesn't just mean a student is answering a question. Other forms of participation might include

- note taking
- nonverbal cues (eye contact, head nodding)
- asking questions
- reacting (laughing, gasping, etc.)
- annotating a text
- debating
- presenting
- playing
- gesturing
- interacting with classmates

When students are engaged in a lesson, they become active participants instead of passive bystanders. And when they are active participants because they are engaged in their learning, they are exponentially more likely to be synthesizing, evaluating, analyzing, and applying.

FOCUSED, EXCITED, AND FULLY ENGAGED STUDENTS

EB Academics has allowed me to create engaging, rigorous, and successful learning experiences for my 6th grade students. An example of this is the "Bountiful Case Activity." It was game changing! I created a "movie trailer" and special "Hollywood style" professional invitation to recruit all willing "detectives" to help me solve the mystery. I rolled them out for two weeks prior to the beginning lesson. The anticipation and excitement built every day! Their discussions were hilarious and they were on edge! I appeared in full detective gear, holding a "case file" in front of my face as we began the actual activity. The engagement was unreal! They were focused, excited, and fully engaged. —*Kala Aguado*

Connecting with the Content

I, Jessica, am not a football fan (though I definitely love baseball), and even though I grew up listening to my dad and brother discuss players' and teams' statistics, it all went in one ear and out the other. Why? Because I had no connection to the sport itself. I did not play it, nor did I watch it on TV. But in 1995, when I was in middle school, my hometown team, the San Francisco 49ers, defeated the San Diego Chargers in the Super Bowl. It was impossible not to get caught up in the hype and excitement of this event. I couldn't help but feel connected to the thousands of fans in the city cheering for Steve Young and the rest of the team. I was engaged in the festivities leading up to the game (Red and Gold Spirit Days at school, friendly bets with family members, etc.). It seemed like everywhere I went in San Francisco, everyone I met had 49ers fever, and I happily became a fan, even if for just a short period of time.

In the weeks following the game, my brother and I delighted in the parody that seemed to play daily on all our local radio stations. Sung to the melody of the ridiculous Christmas song "Grandma Got Run Over by a Reindeer," the lyrics were "Chargers got run over by the Niners at the Super Bowl in Miami. . . ."

Those memories came flooding back to me more than twenty years later, when I was at a local trivia night with my husband and some friends. Now when it comes to trivia, my expertise lies in topics related to early-2000s reality TV. Other than that, I am not too dependable. However, on this particular night, round two was all about sports. My team had pretty much counted me out for any help. And then the host called out this question: "Name two football teams from the same state who have played against each other in the Super Bowl." My husband and friends were debating back and forth over the answer.

Suddenly I began humming. *Chargers got run over by the Niners at the Super Bowl in Miami. . . .*

"I know this! It's the 49ers and the Chargers," I adamantly told my trivia team. "I am one hundred percent certain." Although they doubted me for a few seconds, when I quickly explained how I knew this was true, they accepted my answer. Of course it was correct, and we got the points that round.

Clearly I had connected with that ridiculous parody and was engaged in all things Super Bowl 1995—knowledge that had come in handy (albeit in an unimportant trivia game, but still!) more than twenty years later. Had I not been so engaged and interested in that sporting event, would I have connected to it so strongly? And without a connection to that particular Super Bowl, would I have learned anything about it? (Can I even identify two other football teams that have played against each other in any other Super Bowl? Nope!)

We've all probably experienced difficulty learning something that didn't connect to our personal interests or needs. If there is no engagement on the learner's part, it's much more difficult for them to retain the information. You see, there was another possible answer to that trivia question: the New York Giants and the Buffalo Bills, both NFL teams hailing from the same state, played against each other in the 1991 Super Bowl. I don't think I even knew there was a football team called the Buffalo Bills. Because I had no interest in football, and no connection to the Giants or the Bills, that Super Bowl carried no relevance for me, and thus no learning occurred.

As middle school ELA teachers, we must strive to get our students to engage in our curriculum so that they can connect with the content. Because when they do, they are invested in their learning and retain the information longer.

Engaging Lesson Ideas

In this section, we're going to walk you through some of our favorite engaging lesson ideas to use in the classroom. In the appendix, you will find templates and student directions for many of these activities, so you can take these lessons and adapt them to fit your needs.

For some lesson ideas, we're providing you with the exact activity, and for others, we are giving you an overview of a lesson we used, with the hope that it inspires you to create content that fits your particular curriculum.

Games

An abundance of games can be easily adapted to use with ELA content to increase engagement. The beauty of these games is that they can be used in a variety of ways: at the start of a unit, as a center activity, as an activity for early finishers, as a review for students who are struggling with a concept, as a last-minute sub activity, etc.

READY TO USE FOR THE CLASSROOM

Connotation Concentration

STANDARDS ADDRESSED: Common Core State Standard for ELA Reading for Literature 5.4: Determine the meaning of words and phrases as they are used in a text, including figurative language such as metaphors and similes, and Reading for Literature 6.4: Determine the meaning of words and phrases as they are used in a text, including figurative and connotative meanings; analyze the impact of a specific word choice on meaning and tone.

Connotation Concentration, a game that you can use in your classroom immediately, requires students to identify and match examples of connotative language. It makes a great introduction activity to hook students before they analyze connotative language in a given text and its impact on the text's tone (a key middle school ELA standard). Students will enjoy the competitive aspect of the game as they master connotative language.

To understand how the game works, see the directions for students and the entire lesson plan in the appendix for you to use in your classroom.

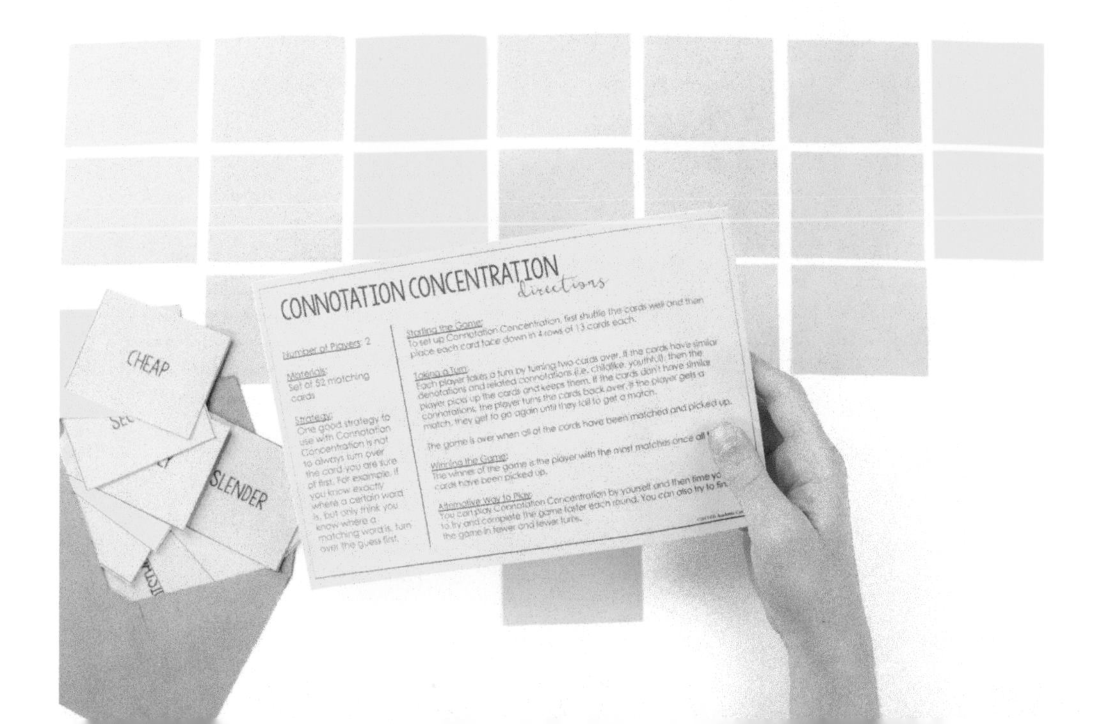

INSPIRATION FOR THE CLASSROOM

Groovy Grammar Games: Pronouns

STANDARDS ADDRESSED: Common Core State Standard for ELA
Language 6.1: Ensure that pronouns are in the proper case (subjective, objective, possessive).

The purpose of this particular game is to help students have fun learning pronouns through a lively card game.

For this game, we prepared sixty game cards, student directions, and an exit ticket for students to demonstrate their understanding of the objective.

To explain how this game works, we've included in the appendix the student directions as well as an assortment of the actual game cards students would use.

APPLICATION IN YOUR CLASSROOM

Now that you've read through the directions of this game as well as seen our entire lesson plan for Connotation Concentration, it's time to brainstorm some games you could adapt for use in your middle school ELA classroom.

Follow these steps to start brainstorming:

1. List any games you enjoy playing, whether they are card or board games. These will serve as inspiration when you design your own ELA games.
2. Choose an ELA standard to focus on. If this is your first time creating an ELA game, we suggest choosing a language standard that focuses on one particular grammatical concept. This will help you remain focused, because those standards are so specific.
3. Determine if any of the games on your list would be a good match for the standard you chose. For example, one of our favorite games is the card game War. The object of that game is to defeat your opponent by having the higher card. You can easily adapt this game for students when practicing tonal words. Since tonal words are categorized as positive, negative, or neutral, a positive word would beat a negative or neutral word, while two neutral cards would result in a war.

Classroom Transformations

Jessica here. As a little kid, I loved the day after Thanksgiving, when my family and I would bring home the Christmas tree we cut down from the local tree farm. We would spend time stringing lights, hanging ornaments, and listening to Christmas music. My dad and I would hang red bows on the banisters leading up our front steps, and my mom would make simple evergreen wreaths to hang on the doors. Then each morning leading up to Christmas Day, my mom

would simmer mulling spices on the stove and play the *Home Alone* soundtrack as my brother and I ate breakfast and got ready for school. Our entire house was transformed. I *lived* for this time of year! The holiday decorations not only lit up my childhood home, but also created special memories for me that continue to this day. Now I carry on the same traditions with my own children, and much to my husband's annoyance, I start the Christmas songs *way* before Thanksgiving (like, waaaaayyyy before).

Take a minute and think about any time your personal space is decorated—whether it's for the holidays, a birthday party, a baby or wedding shower, or the first day of fall. How does the transformed space change the way you feel and act?

The same dynamic holds for the classroom. When we take the time to create classroom transformations, whether they're simple or elaborate, something magical happens. Our students are instantly aware that something different and exciting is happening. And that excitement creates immediate buy-in for the upcoming lesson. In this chapter, we're going to walk you through some classroom transformations we've used to enhance our ELA lessons, and then we're going to brainstorm ways you can use transformations in your own classroom.

Caitlin did a super-simple classroom transformation when her students were reading *Romeo and Juliet.* While she wanted to celebrate the wedding of the two lovebirds, it was important to her that she didn't spend too much time or money putting the celebration together. So she figured, *Why not ask my students for help?* That's just what she did. Each student in the class volunteered to bring in a specific prop or food or costume to stage the wedding. Students brought everything in the day before the wedding was to happen, and Caitlin spent ten minutes before the start of class setting everything up. It was a huge hit and success, and her 8th graders walked away excited to see what would unfold next in the tragic love story.

READY TO USE FOR THE CLASSROOM

Grammar State Fair Boot Camp

STANDARDS ADDRESSED: Common Core State Standard for ELA

Language 5.1: Demonstrate command of the conventions of standard English grammar and usage when writing or speaking.

a. Explain the functions of conjunctions, prepositions, and interjections in general and their function in particular sentences.
b. Form and use the perfect verb tenses.
c. Use verb tense to convey various times, sequences, states, and conditions.
d. Recognize and correct inappropriate shifts in verb tense.
e. Use correlative conjunctions.

Language 6.1: Demonstrate command of the conventions of standard English grammar and usage when writing or speaking.

a. Ensure that pronouns are in the proper case (subjective, objective, possessive).
b. Use intensive pronouns.
c. Recognize and correct inappropriate shifts in pronoun number and person.
d. Recognize and correct vague pronouns (i.e., ones with unclear or ambiguous antecedents).

We knew our students needed to review grammar concepts such as prepositions, conjunctions, interjections, verb tenses, and pronouns before we could move into more complicated grammar concepts later in the year. We didn't want to just give them worksheet after worksheet of grammar drills, so we decided to create a grammar boot camp where they could practice these concepts in an engaging way.

With this activity, teachers transform their classroom into a fair, complete with tickets, images of Ferris wheels, and signs leading to various games. Heck, you could even bring in popcorn or cotton candy for this lesson and hang bunting from your board, like some of the teachers we know did. To build anticipation, we gave our students tickets to the fair in advance, which got them excited to come to ELA class later that week.

On the first day of the fair, students rotated through different stations and participated in practice grammar activities that would help them compete in the grammar games to come.

The following day, students rotated through various grammar fair games: Ring Toss (where they identified coordinating conjunctions, interjections, and pronouns); Pie-Eating Contest (where they combined sentences using correlative conjunctions); Whac-a-Verb (where they completed sentences using a variety of verb tenses); Balloon Darts (where they added various pronouns to incomplete sentences); and Bumper Cars (where they completed a sentence using an appropriate interjection).

Finally, using all the grammar skills they'd mastered, students applied their learning through an authentic writing task. They wrote a postcard to a family member or friend, describing their experiences at the fair and incorporating all of the grammar skills they had studied.

In order to help you bring this high-engagement activity into your classroom, in the appendix we've included our Grammar State Fair Games for you to photocopy and use.

WHO KNEW GRAMMAR COULD BE SO FUN!

Let's just say that I'm not a fan of grammar. It's my weak link. So when I saw the content of this [Grammar State Fair lesson], I knew it was for me! For starters, I generated quite a bit of interest when I ran around to the homerooms on Day One passing out the state fair tickets. I told the students not to lose it. They were so inquisitive about what it was for, but I refused to tell them. It drove them nuts, but kept their interest because every day they didn't know what to expect at the fair. Students' engagement remained high as they worked with a partner on their language standards while playing fair games. This was such a fun unit! Who knew grammar could be so fun [and] be engaging and rigorous for both teachers and students! *—Julie Frey*

INSPIRATION FOR THE CLASSROOM

V.I.P. Game Show

STANDARDS ADDRESSED: Common Core State Standard for ELA

Language 5.2: Demonstrate command of the conventions of standard English capitalization, punctuation, and spelling when writing.

a. Use punctuation to separate items in a series.
b. Use a comma to separate an introductory element from the rest of the sentence.
c. Use a comma to set off the words yes and no, to set off a tag question from the rest of the sentence, and to indicate direct address.
d. Use underlining, quotation marks, or italics to indicate titles of works.

Language 6.2: Demonstrate command of the conventions of standard English capitalization, punctuation, and spelling when writing.

a. Use punctuation (commas, parentheses, dashes) to set off nonrestrictive/parenthetical elements.

When we needed to create some lessons around basic punctuation rules—end marks, capitalization, commas, quotation marks, italics, parentheses, and dashes—we knew we had to make this (frankly dull) topic more engaging. So we decided to have students complete an All Access Pass of punctuation to be on the game show V.I.P. (Very Important Punctuation).

We created signs to hang around the room, letting students know they were on a "soundstage," and even encouraged teachers to use a hairbrush for a microphone as they took on the role of game show host. Of course, our game show needed a theme song, which was easy enough to find with a quick online search.

Students were the contestants, and the grand prize was a dream vacation to Rio de Janeiro, Brazil, which gave us the chance to create another classroom transformation. For this part of the lesson, students would be "traveling around Rio," reading passages about popular tourist destinations; the passages included the punctuation rules they had just reviewed. So we simply included large images of each location to be hung up at the different stations. Finally, students created travel blogs, applying the grammatical concepts in descriptions of their "vacation."

APPLICATION IN YOUR CLASSROOM

Now that you've read through some examples and seen some pictures of classroom transformations, you're probably feeling one of two things: pumped to try a classroom transformation of your own or dread at the thought of doing one.

Keep in mind that a transformation can be as simple or elaborate as you wish. Some teachers find it fun to make a special trip to a craft store or browse online and add decorations to their cart; others don't. Whichever way you feel, we encourage you to at least try a classroom transformation. It is incredibly rewarding for your students—and for you, when you witness their reaction.

Let's walk through how you can get started with a classroom transformation.

1. Brainstorm five possible themes for your transformation. Even better, ask your students for ideas!

2. List at least five potential ELA topics you can use for a transformation.

3. Allow yourself a set amount of time to determine how you will connect a transformation to an ELA topic. Choose one of your themes and ELA topics from above, and jot down five potential decorations and/or activities you could do. (This can also include music or video clips.) *Don't* go down a rabbit hole of online searching. This is supposed to be about

taking action, and we all know how easily distracted we can get searching online for ideas. Jot down your ideas here:

4. Reach out to teachers and family members—or even your community, if you're going all out with the transformation—and see if anyone has props and/or decor to donate. List at least five people/local organizations you can contact. (If the thought of this overwhelms you, skip it and commit to finding five images and/or pieces of clip art that you can use for your transformation.)

5. Create a schedule. Actually write out when you are going to do this transformation. Remember, this is all about taking action.

Build up anticipation with your students. If it's a summer camp transformation, start hanging up camp signs a day or two before the actual activities. Don't discuss the decor with your students. Instead, let them draw their own conclusions. They'll build up the excitement without your saying anything! Add to your lesson plans when you will start building the anticipation.

Escape Rooms

Students *love* escape rooms, and if you haven't jumped on the bandwagon yet, now is the perfect time. For this activity, students solve a series of puzzles focused on any ELA content you're covering (e.g., close reading tasks, answering comprehension questions, organizing plot structure, etc.) and work to "escape" the situation you have created. Escape rooms work brilliantly with classroom transformations but are also perfectly engaging completely on their own!

READY TO USE FOR THE CLASSROOM

Literary Analysis Escape Room

STANDARDS ADDRESSED: Common Core State Standard for ELA
Reading for Literature 5.1: Cite the textual evidence that most strongly supports an analysis of what the text says explicitly as well as inferences drawn from the text.

Reading for Literature 5.4: Determine the meaning of words and phrases as they are used in a text, including figurative language such as metaphors and similes.

Reading for Literature 6.1: Cite textual evidence to support analysis of what the text says explicitly as well as inferences drawn from the text.

Reading for Literature 5.4: Determine the meaning of words and phrases as they are used in a text, including figurative and connotative meanings; analyze the impact of specific word choice on meaning and tone.

We wanted our students to practice closely analyzing a text so that they would be more confident evaluating more complex pieces of literature. So we created comprehension and plot-analysis questions centered around a short text. Students worked in groups, playing games and solving puzzles to escape an abandoned house, which tied into the topic of the text (a middle schooler must spend the night in an abandoned house as part of a dare).

To understand how this escape works, go to the appendix, where we've included the entire lesson plan for you to use in your classroom.

If you'd like to extend this lesson, have your students use the mystery message that they uncover at the end of the escape room to write a response to literature. The response should include a claim, a premise, evidence, and justification.

INSPIRATION FOR THE CLASSROOM

Escape from Alcatraz

STANDARDS ADDRESSED: Common Core State Standard for ELA
Reading for Literature 5.5: Explain how a series of chapters, scenes, or stanzas fits together to provide the overall structure of a particular story, drama, or poem.

Reading for Informational Text 5.5: Compare and contrast the overall structure (e.g., chronology, comparison, cause/effect, problem/solution) of events, ideas, concepts, or information in two or more texts.

Reading for Literature 6.5: Analyze how a particular sentence, chapter, scene, or stanza fits into the overall structure of a text and contributes to the development of the theme, setting, or plot.

Reading for Informational Text 6.5: Analyze how a particular sentence, paragraph, chapter, or section fits into the overall structure of a text and contributes to the development of the ideas.

In this particular mini-unit, students compare and contrast fiction and nonfiction texts about the same topic (in this case, escape attempts from Alcatraz). It was only fitting that we turned the lesson into an actual escape room. We passed out "ferry" tickets to each student and told them we were going on a field trip to Alcatraz. Then we hung different images around the classroom: pictures of Alcatraz, signs that showed the ferry schedule, etc. Students had to travel around the room, looking at each image, reading a corresponding passage, and completing an Alcatraz guidebook, before solving puzzles as part of the escape room.

In order to make it off the island before the last ferry left, students had to solve three puzzles. To do so, students would read a fictional and a factual account of an escape from the island, and compare and contrast the passages to solve the puzzles.

APPLICATION IN YOUR CLASSROOM

Creating an escape room is easier than you might think; often you can use content you already have. It's the perfect way to liven up dry material. Ideally, you should implement it at a time during a unit when students can complete their tasks (mostly) independently. Read through each of the steps below, jotting down your ideas for incorporating an escape room in your classroom.

1. Choose a piece of content or skill to review in your escape room.
2. Consider choosing an escape room theme (catching a flight, escaping zombies, etc.). A theme really adds to the fun!
3. Create multiple-choice questions centered around the content or skill you selected. Create puzzles (break numeric codes, navigate a maze to find the right answer, etc.) based on those questions.
4. Build excitement about your upcoming escape room challenge by adding props or teasing the date for the challenge.

BONUS LESSON IDEA

Mock Trial

Jessica here. The first mock trial I ever organized was my second year of teaching. My 4th graders were studying point of view, and like many teachers, I was using the picture book *The True Story of the Three Little Pigs*, by Jon Scieszka, to illustrate the lesson. After comparing the original story of the three pigs to this altered version, I had my students put the wolf on trial. Students took on the role of the defense and prosecution teams. We had witnesses and a judge and, of course, the wolf himself. They were such a fun two class periods; my students were clearly analyzing literature, interpreting point of view, and using evidence from the text. It was honestly a teacher's dream—one of those awesomely fulfilling days when students don't want the lesson to end!

Mock trials are **IDEAL** to use with short stories and novels where there is some kind of **CONFLICT**.

Mock trials are ideal to use with short stories and novels where there is some kind of conflict. They are wonderful opportunities to dig deeper into the literature and have students practice analyzing evidence. We'll walk you through how you can use a mock trial with the short story "The Monkey's Paw," by W. W. Jacobs, the same way we did. If you're not familiar with that spooky story, here's a quick plot summary: The White family is visiting with a guest who has just returned from colonial India with a monkey's paw in his possession. He claims the monkey's paw has the power to grant wishes. In a strange turn of events, Herbert White, the son, dies at the hands of the monkey's paw. We organized a mock trial to determine if Mr. White was guilty of his son's death.

MOCK TRIALS ARE A HIT

"Mrs. Lang, please tell us we get to do more of these?!" To say my students were engaged in "The Monkey's Paw" Mock Trial is an understatement! They still talk about this lesson months later and beg for more. Every student had a specific role and things they needed to complete to make the trial work. This was incredibly motivating for my students because they wanted their team to win the trial. And yet, while they each had a responsibility, the students were able to collaborate and work together. It was even a success with my most challenging class! [This] has proven to me that students can handle rigorous material when engagement is at the forefront of the lesson plan. —*Sarah Lang*

APPLICATION IN YOUR CLASSROOM

1. Divide students into three teams (prosecution, defense, and jury).
2. Provide students with Prosecution Team Handouts and Defense Team Handouts that clearly define the expectations for everyone's role (these handouts are included in the appendix for you). Each team member should have a handout specific to their role and what they are working on for the trial. Here is a picture of what a handout might look like for the member of the prosecution team in charge of the opening statement:

3. Consider what you would like the members of the jury to work on while the prosecution and defense teams are preparing their statements and evidence. You may wish to have these students search for evidence in the text that supports either a guilty or an innocent verdict, in preparation for the trial.
4. On the day of the trial, arrange your classroom like a courtroom, with separate places for the three teams (prosecution, defense, and jury) and a place for you to sit at the front. You can even go an extra step and decorate your classroom with court-themed signs. Some of our EB Teachers' Club members had their students dress in "courtroom attire" during their mock trials, which further increased engagement and made the day extra special. One teacher even had a local law enforcement official visit the class and observe the trial. He had prepared ahead of time and read the short story "The Monkey's Paw" in anticipation of his visit! How cool is that?

5. As the judge, decide what punishment you will issue in case the defendant (the character from the text) is found guilty. You will need to be prepared to announce this during the sentencing if necessary.
6. Follow a clear agenda for the mock trial so the class period runs smoothly and all students know what to expect.
7. To ensure the highest level of engagement, encourage students not to read word for word from their handouts. They should attempt to get into character, maintain eye contact with the jury, and speak with expression. (You can see how encouraging students to dress up on the day of the trial may help them step into their role.)
8. Provide the jury with a verdict template to complete as they deliberate the facts of the case. This way they have an organized and prepared statement to read to the court at the appropriate time.

With any activity like this, we always recommend having students fill out a reflection sheet to determine what worked well and what can be improved for future activities.

Things to consider when using a mock trial for a piece of literature:

1. Include a discussion with your students (and provide them with background knowledge) about trials and their purpose. This is important, because students will need to understand the roles individuals play in a trial (prosecution, defense, etc.), since they will be filling one of those roles.
2. Choose a text in which a character performs an action that can be debated and the consequences analyzed. Then create an essential question centered around that character. Let your students know that this is the question they will be arguing in court. If you share this with students *before* they begin reading the text, then they can use it as a lens through which they read as they search for evidence to support either side of the answer.
3. Read and annotate the text together, modeling for students (at first) how to find evidence to support either side of your essential question. Providing students with an evidence tracker to organize all their evidence can help set them up for success with this activity.

4. If you can, allow students to indicate their preference for what role they would like in the trial. If you're able to accommodate students' preferences, they may be even more engaged.

The ideas we've shared in this chapter are just a few of the many engaging lessons that can be used in your classroom. But it is paramount to remember that engagement is just one component that allows you to step into the role of an empowered middle school ELA teacher. If you just have engagement, everyone may be having fun, but unless rigor is present too, how are you going to get your students mastering the ELA standards? You need a planning framework to rely on as you create these lessons, to make sure that they are actually covering the material your students need to master.

In the next chapter, we'll explore how to elevate the rigor in your classroom, and how already having the engagement factor in place will help your students rise to higher expectations.

Chapter 4:

THE IMPORTANCE OF RIGOR

Why Even Incorporate Rigor?

Rigor can be a tricky topic. As middle school ELA teachers, we want to challenge our students and help them grow as critical readers and writers. We do this by exposing them to reading and writing opportunities that increase in complexity as the year progresses. Yet so often we hear teachers saying, whether in the classroom or in ELA Facebook groups, "My students can't handle that [fill in the assignment of your choice]. They're only 6th graders." Or, "My class can't write an evidence-based essay. They can't even write a paragraph."

But could it be that these limiting beliefs are holding our students back from what they are truly capable of? Are we missing out on opportunities to incorporate more rigor into our lessons because we're underestimating our students' capacity for learning? We believe that the answer to both of these questions is often yes.

> What if instead of **ASSUMING** a piece of literature or a writing assignment is just too hard for our students, we created lessons stemming from the mindset that our students' **SUCCESS** is inevitable?

Jessica here. In the midst of the 2020 pandemic, when school as we knew it was completely upended, my husband and I decided that I would homeschool our second grader, Jameson. I found a reading and math curriculum that I liked (definitely engaging and rigorous), and he took an online science class (no way was I going to attempt science experiments on my own each week). As for the writing, as a curriculum developer for EB Academics, I decided he was going to learn our EB Writing Approach (evidence-based writing for literary analysis).

Though the teachers who use this writing approach see awesome results in their students' writing, sometimes they are apprehensive about trying it because they think it will be too hard for their students. When I hear teachers say this, it drives me nuts. Because here was my second grader, using the exact same writing framework that we teach in middle school—the only thing different was the level of the texts I had him read!

I set the expectations high and he crushed it. I'm not saying this to brag about my son. He's a typical kid who will tell you his favorite subject is recess. And we definitely had our battles during homeschool. But by practicing this writing framework *every single week*, he was participating in rigorous lessons that helped him develop writing stamina.

What if instead of assuming a piece of literature or a writing assignment is just too hard for our students, we created lessons stemming from the mindset that our students' success is inevitable? If you knew from the start of an ELA unit that your students were going to master the standards and critically analyze complex topics in both essays and class discussions, how would you show up differently? Would you be scrambling at the last minute to plan out the day's lesson, or would you plan your unit in advance? Would you purposely build in scaffolding activities leading up to a difficult unit, or would you just jump from one unit to the next? Again, knowing your students' success was inevitable, would you try a different approach when things got a little tough? Would you spend an extra day or two on the concept and not stress about fitting in all your standards?

As for Jameson, the first few times he wrote a paragraph that included textual evidence, it was tough and required a lot of hand-holding. But I knew his success was inevitable, and after just a few practice rounds, he wrote this:

> *"Dolphin Day" is a fictional story written by Elodie McNamara. Diego, the dolphin, goes to the Deep Sea Amusement Park. He eats treats and goes on scary rides, but he needs to get home before it gets dark because he is afraid. Diego finds a tiny, little guppy and then he's not afraid anymore. They decide to go back to the park next year and even stay for the fireworks after it gets dark. The character traits that best describe Diego at the beginning and end of the story are scared and brave.*
>
> *At the beginning, Diego is scared. On page 3, he says, "I can't be here after it gets dark. There's too many spooky sharks." At the end of the story Diego is brave because he says to the guppy, "I'm not afraid anymore. Let's go watch the fireworks."*

If a seven-year-old (whose prior writing experience was limited) can write this after just a few lessons, imagine what middle schoolers can do! They are more than capable of reading complex texts and writing multi-paragraph critical essays.

When we approach the idea of rigorous lessons with the mindset of inevitable success, our behaviors change and thus our students' behaviors change. When we step into the role of an empowered ELA teacher, our students rise to the new level of expectations. We naturally push our students further than we thought they were capable of. We witness "lightbulb moments" in our students that show us they can handle the rigor. We start to see them mastering the ELA standards.

In the last chapter we discussed the importance of engagement. In this chapter we're exploring how we can make rigor front and center in our ELA classrooms and have students embracing the work. So let's talk about the concrete steps we can take to make that happen.

Your Road Map (a Standards Checklist)

An empowered ELA teacher doesn't teach lessons they find online just because they look fun. An empowered ELA teacher doesn't just teach straight from a textbook in whatever order the table of contents suggests. Rather, an empowered ELA teacher makes strategic decisions about what to teach and when to teach it based on their students' needs. And in order to make those strategic curriculum decisions, they need a road map.

Just as the captain of a ship would never go out to sea without a compass (or GPS!) for guidance, we can't expect to teach all year without a road map telling us if we are traveling in the right direction. And for teachers, that road map is a standards checklist.

A standards checklist is hands-down one of the most useful tools for incorporating rigorous lessons into your classroom and getting your students to master the standards. It includes all the ELA standards for your grade level, along with columns where you can document the date(s) you've taught the standards and monitor how well your students grasped a particular standard. It's an integral part of the EB Lesson Planning Approach, which we cover in chapter 5.

We print out a standards checklist and keep it on our desk so that we can refer to it whenever we sit down to plan. Any lesson we create must cover at least one standard on the checklist, so we know that we are helping our students progress throughout the school year. If we have an idea for a lesson but we can't

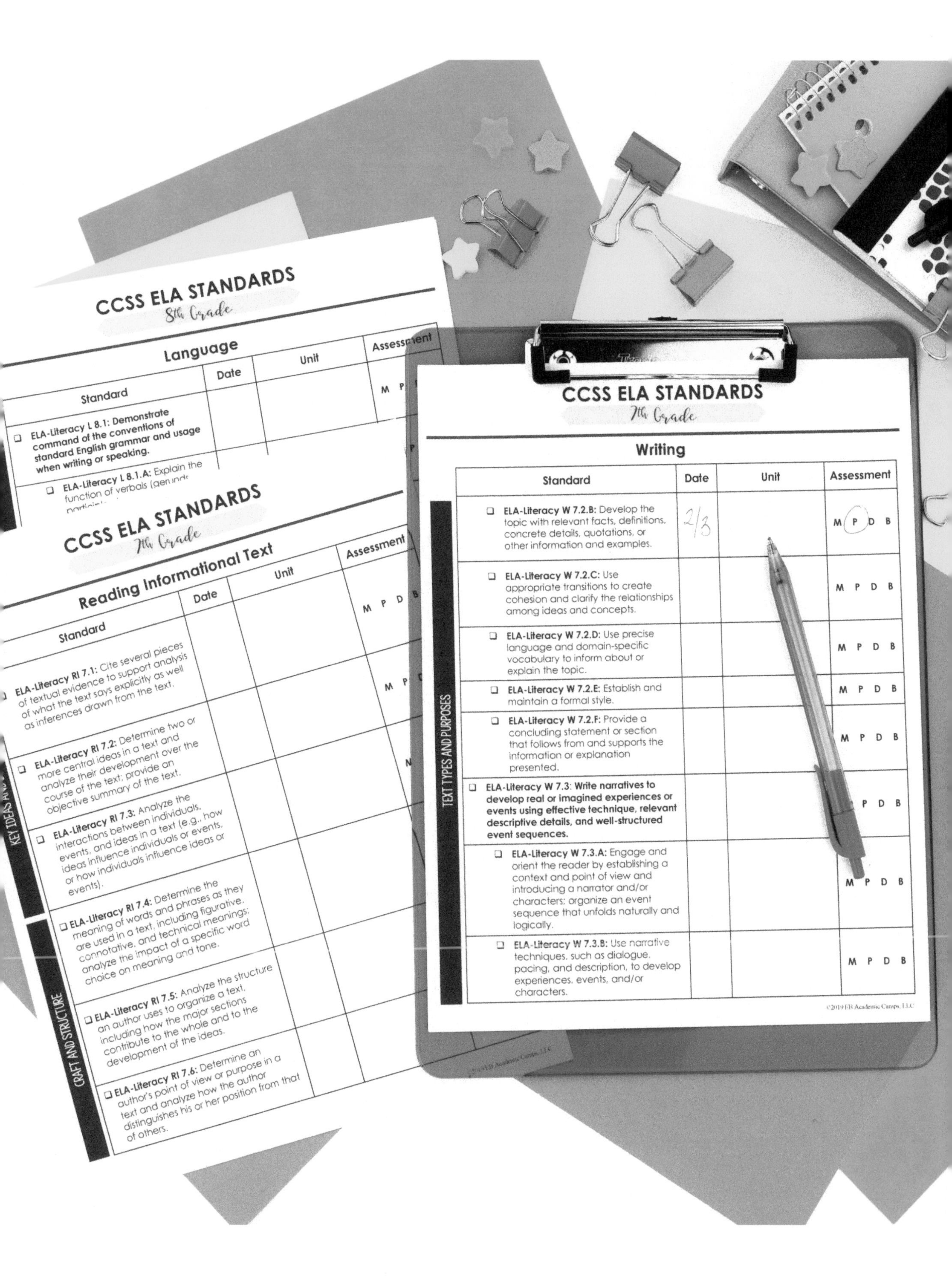
CCSS ELA STANDARDS
8th Grade
Language
Standard
Date
Unit
Assessment
ELA-Literacy L 8.1: Demonstrate command of the conventions of standard English grammar and usage when writing or speaking.
ELA-Literacy L 8.1.A: Explain the function of verbals (gerunds
CCSS ELA STANDARDS
7th Grade
Reading Informational Text
Standard
Date
Unit
Assessment
KEY IDEAS AND
ELA-Literacy RI 7.1: Cite several pieces of textual evidence to support analysis of what the text says explicitly as well as inferences drawn from the text.
ELA-Literacy RI 7.2: Determine two or more central ideas in a text and analyze their development over the course of the text; provide an objective summary of the text.
ELA-Literacy RI 7.3: Analyze the interactions between individuals, events, and ideas in a text (e.g., how ideas influence individuals or events, or how individuals influence ideas or events).
CRAFT AND STRUCTURE
ELA-Literacy RI 7.4: Determine the meaning of words and phrases as they are used in a text, including figurative, connotative, and technical meanings; analyze the impact of a specific word choice on meaning and tone.
ELA-Literacy RI 7.5: Analyze the structure an author uses to organize a text, including how the major sections contribute to the whole and to the development of the ideas.
ELA-Literacy RI 7.6: Determine an author's point of view or purpose in a text and analyze how the author distinguishes his or her position from that of others.
M P D B
CCSS ELA STANDARDS
7th Grade
Writing
Standard
Date
Unit
Assessment
TEXT TYPES AND PURPOSES
ELA-Literacy W 7.2.B: Develop the topic with relevant facts, definitions, concrete details, quotations, or other information and examples.
2/3
M P D B
ELA-Literacy W 7.2.C: Use appropriate transitions to create cohesion and clarify the relationships among ideas and concepts.
M P D B
ELA-Literacy W 7.2.D: Use precise language and domain-specific vocabulary to inform about or explain the topic.
M P D B
ELA-Literacy W 7.2.E: Establish and maintain a formal style.
M P D B
ELA-Literacy W 7.2.F: Provide a concluding statement or section that follows from and supports the information or explanation presented.
M P D B
ELA-Literacy W 7.3: Write narratives to develop real or imagined experiences or events using effective technique, relevant descriptive details, and well-structured event sequences.
P D B
ELA-Literacy W 7.3.A: Engage and orient the reader by establishing a context and point of view and introducing a narrator and/or characters; organize an event sequence that unfolds naturally and logically.
M P D B
ELA-Literacy W 7.3.B: Use narrative techniques, such as dialogue, pacing, and description, to develop experiences, events, and/or characters.
M P D B
©2019 EB Academic Camps, LLC

incorporate a standard, then nine times out of ten we're not doing that lesson.

This is the checklist we use along with our list of inspiring ideas (remember, you brainstormed some ideas in the last chapter) to create engaging and rigorous lessons. Your action item for right now, though, is simply to print out a copy of your grade-level ELA standards and put it front and center on your desk, or wherever you do your planning. We strongly suggest you print a physical copy of it so it's easy for you to access and jot down notes immediately after an ELA unit. If you use a digital copy, it's too easy to forget to refer to it when you're planning and to update it after lessons. Then, once again, you're like a captain without a compass.

Your **ACTION** item for right now is to print out a copy of your grade-level **ELA STANDARDS** and put it front and center on your desk, or wherever you do your planning.

Questioning Your Lessons

We're going to assume you printed out your grade-level ELA standards and they are now sitting on your desk, ready for your next lesson planning session. When you sit down to plan, any activity you create is going to be centered around one or more of those standards—for example, Common Core State Standard for ELA Writing 7.4: "Produce clear and coherent writing in which the development, organization, and style are appropriate to task, purpose, and audience." After you come up with your standards-aligned lesson, we encourage you to use the following questioning method to add more rigor to it.

Here are the questions you may wish to consider:

- What else can I add to this lesson or unit to make it more challenging and in-depth for my students?
- How can I move my students up the "rigor ladder"?
- What activities can I include that encourage my students to synthesize their learning and apply their knowledge to other tasks?

When we step into the role of an empowered ELA teacher, one who embraces these three components of teaching (engagement, rigor, and a lesson planning framework), we must consider that what got us here won't get us there. We may have gotten used to our old way of planning, but at what cost? Did we skip some lessons or question some content because we thought our students weren't capable of handling it? Did we lower our expectations because we were strapped for time and needed to move on to the next unit? If our goal is to get our students mastering the standards and to critically analyze complex texts through both writing and discussion, then we must change our habits and start consistently asking ourselves, *What can I do to elevate the rigor in this lesson?*

Let's say you want to increase the rigor in your study of *Romeo and Juliet.* Perhaps in the past, you had your students simply summarize the different acts and take periodic quizzes. Of course, there's absolutely nothing wrong with having students summarize a text—that activity certainly has its time and place, as it's a skill that students need to master.

However, if you want to increase the rigor for this unit, let's go back to the questions we mentioned above and walk through some possible answers, so you can see this in action.

WHAT ELSE CAN I ADD TO THIS LESSON OR UNIT TO MAKE IT MORE CHALLENGING AND IN-DEPTH FOR MY STUDENTS?

What if for each act, you provided your students with a text-dependent critical-thinking question? Then students could summarize each act (so still practicing that skill!) and develop a robust answer for it. For example, after reading Act V, students might answer a critical-thinking question such as "Who is most responsible for the deaths of Romeo and Juliet?" This requires students to formulate a claim and provide premises, evidence, and justification, which covers a wide array of standards.

HOW CAN I MOVE MY STUDENTS UP THE "RIGOR LADDER"?

If this is a unit you've taught before, you most likely have some comprehension questions that your students will be answering. An easy fix to get students moving up the "rigor ladder" using questions you already have is to make them suitable for use in a Socratic seminar. In this case, the questions must be open-ended and text dependent. For example, if you have the basic comprehension question "How old is Juliet when she marries Romeo?" you could elevate it to "Based on Juliet's age in the play, is true love possible at a young age? Compare Romeo and Juliet's relationship to instances of young love in other literature." Imagine the level of discussion your middle schoolers would have debating this question during a Socratic seminar. That simply isn't possible with the first question about Juliet's age, since there's no room for discussion.

WHAT ACTIVITIES CAN I INCLUDE THAT ENCOURAGE MY STUDENTS TO SYNTHESIZE THEIR LEARNING AND APPLY THEIR KNOWLEDGE TO OTHER TASKS?

Instead of just ending with a typical multiple-choice and short-answer assessment (which is still great and can also be included), what if you added an activity allowing students to not only synthesize their learning, but also apply their knowledge? In this case, you could include a creative culminating project such as a music video. For this project, students come up with a concept for a music video centered around a modern adaptation of the play. They write lyrics to their own song, which must cover the entirety of the play and include elements of rhyme and figurative language and show an understanding of the play's main message(s) and theme(s). To give you a glimpse of the exact project that we used, we've included both the Teacher Instructions for Use as well as the Student Directions Handout in the appendix, so you can use it too.

We hope you can see how using these questions can increase the rigor in your lessons, allowing students to master your grade-level standards.

Adjusting Your Expectations

Earlier in this chapter, we discussed the problem of limiting beliefs about what students are capable of in the classroom. And while we firmly believe we must operate from the mindset that our students' success is inevitable, we realize there are adjustments we must make depending on our students' grade level.

We both taught 5th grade (Jessica for almost ten years, and Caitlin for one), and we both read the short story "The Gift of the Magi" with our students. Many teachers didn't understand why we would purposely use such a complex text with ten- and eleven-year-olds when it was typically taught in 8th or 9th grade. But you know what? Our students thrived with this short story and the high expectations we set for them.

However, we were also practical. Knowing that the text was difficult, we frontloaded students with prereading activities such as Popcorn Predictions (see details on page 99) and vocabulary activities to set them up for success and familiarize them with the story before we read it aloud. We incorporated skits and watched the *Sesame Street* version of the story to help students better grasp the concepts. We provided them with their final essay question *before* we started reading, so we could search for supporting evidence together as we read—a habit we encourage no matter what grade you teach.

In the end, students wrote thoughtful, evidence-based essays arguing which character made the more substantial sacrifice:

ESSAY QUESTION

There are several benefits to providing your students with their final essay question before reading a text:

- The question gives you a lens through which to discuss the text with your students.
- Students can annotate for and find evidence as they read.
- Students engage more closely with the text because they are focused on a specific question.
- Students' final essays are stronger because they can find the perfect piece of evidence through the course of their reading. If they wait until they're writing their essay, they're more likely to randomly choose a quote that may not apply to the prompt. (In some cases, by the time students sit down to write, they don't even remember those perfect pieces of evidence.)

Jim, who sold his watch, or Della, who sold her hair. (If you're not familiar with this story, Jim and Della are an impoverished married couple who selflessly give up their most prized possessions to purchase gifts for each other. Jim peddles his gold watch, which had been passed down through the generations, to purchase hair combs for Della, who sells her hair to buy a platinum watch chain for Jim.)

Overall, we adjusted our expectations for how the literature unit would look with our students. We didn't use an abridged text or shy away from a difficult text. Instead we helped our students better grasp the material by providing them with intentional scaffolding activities. We extended the unit and spent more time reading and discussing the text, not feeling pressured to check off the standards we were covering and move on to the next topic. And because we were so confident and familiar with our 5th grade ELA standards (since we used that standards checklist to plan), our expectations for their final essays were different than what an 8th grade teacher would be looking for in their students' writing.

And if those 5th graders happen to encounter that story again when they are older, think of the schema they will already have in place to bring to the discussion. Think about how much more deeply they will be able to analyze themes that may not have been a central focus during their 5th grade unit on the story.

STUDENTS WILL EXCEED YOUR EXPECTATIONS

I am in my ninth year of teaching, and I'm always looking for fun and rigorous ways to engage my students. A favorite activity of my 7th graders [was] the Bountiful Case [an unsolved whodunnit mystery lesson]. My students [were] completely engrossed in the mystery. The structure of the activity had them using academic vocabulary and not only making claims and spouting off theories, but supporting their theories with logical reasoning and evidence. Based on their inferences, students participated in a lively discussion that went beyond my expectations. *—Kate Waggoner*

Rigor and Differentiation

Adjusting expectations may also mean differentiating within your own classroom to best meet your students' needs. We'd be willing to bet that you've attended differentiation training at some point in your teaching career. Sometimes the ideas and strategies shared in those trainings can seem daunting to implement if you're the only adult in your classroom during ELA lessons.

One simple strategy to help provide differentiation to students when reading complex texts (and perhaps writing an evidence-based essay about a challenging topic) is to give different graphic organizers to your students. The expectation (a completed evidence-based essay) is still the same for each student, but the path to get there may be different.

Using the same writing prompt we gave our 5th graders for "The Gift of the Magi," take a look at the different introductory paragraph organizers we may provide for various groups of students. Recall that the essay prompt we used was "Who makes the larger sacrifice? Jim selling his gold watch or Della selling her hair?"

Assuming you've already taught your students a common writing framework, your differentiated graphic organizers may look something like this:

Struggling Writers:

- Write a TAG (title, author, and genre) for "The Gift of the Magi" on this line (one sentence):
- Write a summary (Somebody . . . wanted . . . but . . . so . . . then . . .) for the story on this line (two sentences):
- Write a claim (your answer to the question "Who makes the larger sacrifice, Jim or Della?") on this line (one sentence):

On-Level Writers:

- TAG (one sentence)
- Summary (two to three sentences)
- Claim (one sentence)

Advanced Writers:

- Write an introductory paragraph that includes a TAG that connects to your summary and a claim that does not include personal pronouns.
- Make sure to use at least three adjectives and one academic vocabulary word from this unit in your paragraph.

Name ______________________ Date __________

Response to Literature Graphic Organizer

introductory paragraph

Write a **TAG** (title, author, and genre) for "The Gift of the Magi" (one sentence):

(indent) ______________________

____

Write a **SUMMARY** (Somebody... wanted... but... so... then...) for the story (two sentences):

____

____

____

Write a **CLAIM** (This is your answer to the question "Who makes the larger sacrifice, Jim or Della?") (one sentence):

____

____

Name ______________________ Date __________

Response to Literature Graphic Organizer

introductory paragraph

TAG (one sentence):

____

____

SUMMARY (two to three sentences):

____

____

____

CLAIM (one sentence):

____

____

Name ______________________ Date ____________

Response to Literature Graphic Organizer

introductory paragraph

Write an introductory paragraph below. Be sure to include a TAG that connects to your summary and a claim. Be sure to use at least three adjectives and one academic vocabulary word in your paragraph.

Yes, it takes a bit more prep up front to create a few different graphic organizers (honestly, just some cutting and pasting of extra hints), but once you've created them, you're all set for any time you teach that particular text. You're not juggling different stories and multiple essay prompts. Instead you're adjusting your expectations for how students approach their writing assessment, while still providing the rigor!

Rigor and Spiraling Your Curriculum

When I, Jessica, would sit down each night to do homework with my oldest son, Jameson, he typically had to complete a math workbook page with a few problems about whatever concept he was learning (for instance, subtracting two-digit numbers), and at the bottom of the page, there would be two or three review questions on a concept he had covered months ago. I loved it. What a quick and easy way to spiral the math curriculum to ensure students retain past concepts. It's such a simple approach, and it seems to naturally occur in math class. But from our experience, spiraling ELA curriculum isn't as common. And it sure as heck should be!

SPIRALING ELA CURRICULUM:

This occurs when you do a "deep dive" of a particular ELA concept or standard and then periodically revisit it throughout the year, so that students master the standard.

Check in with yourself. Have you ever taught a particular type of writing (narrative, expository, persuasive, etc.), and then once you graded your students' final writing piece, you moved on to the next unit and never revisited that first type of writing? That's how we used to teach writing too; it's incredibly common for ELA teachers to teach writing units in isolation and only cover them once. Or maybe after you teach a particular grammar concept and have the assessment, you don't practice that skill again. We get it. There are a whole lot of ELA standards to cover, and there's not a lot of time in your schedule.

But when you intentionally spiral your ELA curriculum, you naturally incorporate more rigor into your lessons and nudge students closer to mastering the standards.

Here's what this might look like:

You teach a deep-dive narrative writing unit at the beginning of the year. We're talking leads, endings, dialogue, transitions, word choice, etc. Students write their final narrative piece incorporating all the narrative concepts you taught during your deep dive.

A month goes by. It's almost Halloween. What a perfect time for students to write three different spooky-themed leads that could be used for a narrative. They don't have to write a full-blown narrative, just the leads, so we're looking at one class period of time and you're already spiraling in your narrative writing unit. To elevate the lesson, perhaps you have students include examples of figurative language that they've been learning about.

Another month goes by, and you spend one class period reviewing dialogue rules in writing. This time students must also include simple, compound, and complex sentences in their dialogue, because you're going to spiral in some grammar review as well.

Notice how the activities get more rigorous as they are spiraled into the year! Think of the benefits of spiraling your curriculum this way:

- Students are more likely to master your grade-level ELA standards because they are continually practicing the concepts.

- You are able to incorporate more complex activities because students are slowly weaving in the different concepts they've learned.
- Your scope and sequence for the year is more organized and intentional because you are planning out your activities way in advance. (No joke, when we batch planned our lessons in the summer, we'd pencil in our narrative unit in August/September and then flip to one day for each subsequent month and schedule in a narrative writing review activity! It was wonderful seeing days in our scope and sequence completely filled months in advance. More on batch planning later . . . it's a game changer!)
- This alleviates much of the pressure you might feel to get your students to master the standards during one particular unit.

In order to be as **EFFECTIVE** teachers as we can be, we must strive to include **RIGOR** in our ELA lessons.

Hopefully, you're on board! In order to be the most effective teachers we can be, we must strive to include rigor in our ELA lessons. And of course, we know the benefits (outlined in chapter 3) for utilizing engaging lessons! When you combine rigor and engagement in the classroom, you are well on your way to success. But if you're reading this and thinking, *This sounds awesome for my students but like a* whole *lot of work for me,* then this next chapter, where we dive into the final component of the EB Lesson Planning Approach, will be a game changer. We are going all in on the single most effective way to plan these engaging and rigorous lessons, so that you aren't spending your nights and weekends knee-deep in literature anthologies and Pinterest searches. Instead you'll be enjoying brunch with friends, binge-watching the latest Netflix obsession, or spending quality time with your kids, resting easy knowing that your lessons are *done* for the next few months. Start thinking about what your dream work-free weekend might look like, because we're going to help you achieve it!

Weekly Planner
Weekly Planner

Chapter 5:

YOUR LESSON PLANNING APPROACH

WE DON'T KNOW about you, but with all the classes we took in preparation for becoming middle school ELA teachers, there was never a class on lesson planning. It was up to us to figure out our planning approach as we went along. And for the first couple of years in the classroom, it looked something like this (Caitlin's experience speaks for both of us):

> Prep period would roll around on Thursday afternoon, when my students went to art and PE. After answering parent emails, grading the rest of *The House on Mango Street* essays that I'd been meaning to get to, and making copies for the next day's chapter 7 vocabulary quizzes, I had only fifteen minutes left to plan. So I'd open the class literature anthology to see what story was next; search Pinterest for "engaging lesson ideas for 'Thank You, M'am'"; scroll through Teachers Pay Teachers, looking for "Thank You, M'am" short story units; and read through descriptions of units, wondering if they would work for my students. And then the bell would ring and the class would come back for the last period of the day.
>
> So on Friday afternoon, I would lug my teacher bag home with teacher's editions, my planning book, and the chapter 7 vocabulary quizzes to grade. And all day Saturday, the bag would sit by the door, as if taunting me whenever I walked by it, a constant reminder of what Sunday afternoon would bring.
>
> Sunday would roll around, and while my husband watched football and my friends met up for brunch, I would drag the dreaded teacher bag to the kitchen table, spread everything out, and settle in for four or five hours of planning and more Pinterest searches for "Thank You, M'am" units, silently cursing Roger and Mrs. Luella Bates Washington Jones and thinking, *If my students only knew how much time I put into each lesson as they roll their eyes and groan when I assign an essay . . .*

It wasn't until we were several years into teaching and after lots of trial and error that we developed a planning framework that actually worked. No more endless searches down the online rabbit hole. No more lugging a teacher

When you know your ELA lessons must be **ENGAGING** and **RIGOROUS** and you actually have a **PLAN** for creating them, you are **UNSTOPPABLE**.

bag home every Friday—in fact, we got rid of the bag! No more Sunday Scaries and waking up dreading an entire afternoon spent lesson planning while everyone else lay around watching the game and enjoying seven-layer dip.

Nope. This lesson planning approach, which we call the EB Lesson Planning Approach, put a stop to all of that. And once we started lesson planning in the way we are going to break down for you, there were a whole lot of positive ripple effects:

- Walking into class each Monday totally prepared and excited to teach because all our plans were completely ready to go—not just for the upcoming week, but for the next few months. (Wait, *what*?)
- Avoiding waiting in line to make those last-minute copies we needed. (Our copies were done for the next few weeks!)
- Having fun on the weekend and not thinking about school . . . getting that much-needed pedicure, binge-watching our latest guilty pleasure, reading for fun, working out. (All right, that last one might be pushing it!)
- Watching classroom-management and behavior issues diminish because we were so organized with our plans that our students knew *exactly* what was expected of them each day and started taking ownership in their learning. (There was no downtime for getting in trouble!)
- Actually watching a movie with our husbands and not having fifteen computer tabs open on our laptops and our lesson plan books sprawled across our laps.

Sounds pretty good, right?

Implementing the EB Lesson Planning Approach is the third component in the process of becoming an empowered ELA teacher. Because when you know your ELA lessons must be engaging and rigorous and you actually have a plan for creating them, you are unstoppable. That's when you and your students will *Thrive*.

This is when the other teachers at your school start asking you, "What's your secret? Why do all the kids love being in your class? How do you have the best writers? How are you able to leave at 3:00 p.m. each day?" This is when you no longer dread an impromptu visit (or a scheduled one!) from your principal, because you know you are rocking your lessons. And it all comes back to the EB Lesson Planning Approach.

When we talk about the importance of having a lesson planning approach, we mean knowing *how* to plan, *what* to plan, and *when* to plan.

The *how* is the actual planning approach we're going to share with you.

The *what* is the actual content you are going to teach and list in your plans. Is it an activity, a close reading assignment, a quiz, a response to literature? The *what* always ties back to the standards—remember those standards checklists we raved about back in chapter 4? They are critical for the EB Lesson Planning Approach.

The *when* might just be our favorite part of this approach. We're going to share with you how we and thousands of the teachers inside the EB Teachers' Club batch plan so that we can leave school when the bell rings and don't have to touch our plan books over the weekend.

This section is all about *how* to plan those engaging and rigorous lessons you'll be using in your ELA classroom.

We're about to dive into the EB Lesson Planning Approach so you can start putting it into place and see awesome results. But before we do, we want to lay the foundations for you. That way you know where you're going on this lesson planning journey we're about to take you on.

Our EB Lesson Planning Approach consists of four important aspects:

- batch planning your lessons
- using a scope and sequence
- making the ELA standards your guide
- using our Into, Through, and Beyond Framework to backwards plan

If any of this makes you nervous, hang with us. Because the moment you incorporate these four aspects into your own planning, you'll start to experience a classroom where students are having fun and mastering the standards, all without your sacrificing your nights and weekends to plan.

GONE ARE THE WEEKDAYS AND WEEKENDS SPENT PLANNING

I was the teacher who would stay three hours at school every Monday and Friday to grade and still work until 8 p.m. every Tuesday and Thursday to finish grading and plan my lessons for the next week. I was that teacher who the staff needed to kick out of the school for staying too long. Since becoming an EB Teacher, I no longer stay three hours, and I have taken [on a] love for batch planning. Not only that, I can spend time with my kids so much more than ever before. We can now do crafts, play hide and seek, and go to the playground all in one week, unlike before when we could only do one fun activity, and it had to be on a Saturday. Gone are those days! I can be a fun mommy again. *—Frauline Walker*

Do. Now would be a good time to describe what a perfect work-free weekend looks like for you, since all your planning is going to be done for the upcoming weeks, or even months. Go ahead and write down your perfect weekend here—or dream even bigger! What other hobbies, goals, and pursuits outside of teaching would you like to have more time to explore?

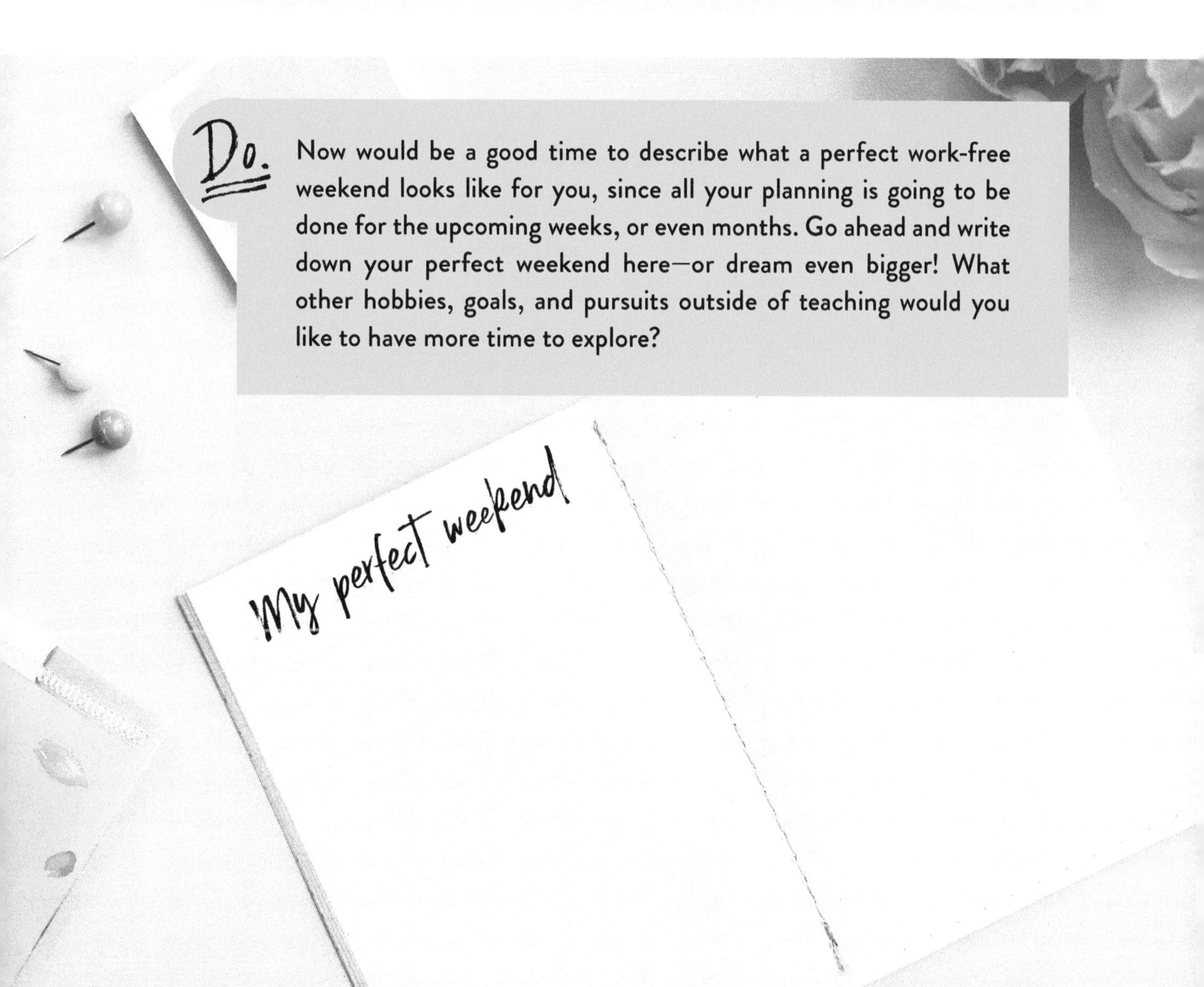

Because when you have the destination in mind, all the work you do up front makes it so worth it. You can reread this wish list of what you're working toward when you sit down to implement the EB Lesson Planning Approach. Even better, once you implement the EB Lesson Planning Approach, there's nothing stopping you from having work-free weekends to pursue these goals and ideas and activities!

STUCK ON WHAT WORK-FREE WEEKENDS ACTUALLY LOOK LIKE? NEED SOME INSPIRATION?

JESSICA'S PERFECT WORK-FREE WEEKENDS: Sleep past 6:30 a.m. Go on a run while listening to a *This American Life* podcast. Drive across the Golden Gate Bridge with my husband and kids and eat the Tuscan White Bean and Tuna Salad at Fish while watching the boats return to the harbor. Meet up with a small group of friends for a glass of wine (preferably at the wine bar around the corner). Be snuggled in bed and watching a movie by 8:00 p.m.

CAITLIN'S PERFECT WORK-FREE WEEKENDS: Sleep until 7:00 a.m. Get my son, Will, ready for the day while my husband, Bob, makes eggs and toasted sourdough bread. Spend the morning on a bike ride together around town, then head to a quick lunch at our local burger joint. Back home at naptime for Will and an uninterrupted workout for me. Take an evening walk through town with our two dogs, Charlie and Huckleberry, getting home in time to cook up a delicious dinner with a glass of full-bodied red wine. Will goes to bed, and Bob and I spend time watching a documentary together before falling fast asleep by 10:30 p.m.

All right, now that you have a perfect work-free weekend in mind, let's dive a little deeper into the four components of the EB Lesson Planning Approach.

Batch Planning

When I, Caitlin, first started teaching, I was that teacher that we mentioned earlier—always working on the weekends, searching frantically online the night before to find a decent lesson on tomorrow's topic.

It was constant survival mode. And honestly, I didn't really know there was a better way until I realized that I *needed* a better way if I wanted to be able to continue to teach and be excited to show up to school every day.

Teacher burnout is *real*.

The first time I realized that something needed to change was in 2013, when I returned to the classroom after a year-long hiatus in the corporate world. (This was the same year that Jessica and I taught across the hall from each other.) I realized if I were going to remain in the classroom (which is truly where I wanted to be), I couldn't work the same hours that I did those first few years of teaching.

So, as Jessica had done with her own planning, I decided to sit down for a few days and plan out my entire year for both my 7th and 8th grade ELA curriculums. Every grammar concept, every set of vocabulary words, every Socratic seminar discussion, every test—*everything* was planned to a T. By planning everything in advance, my goal was to leave school by 3:30, not bring work home with me, and have a life where I wasn't constantly in school mode even when I wasn't at school. All of a sudden, brunch with my friends on the weekend and walking my dogs along the beach on a Tuesday afternoon were not only possible, but the norm.

Even though this was my first year teaching middle school after having taught high school for four years prior, because of my detailed year-long plans, I had never felt more prepared and more importantly, more confident to take on a school year. I knew on any given day exactly what I would be teaching and why.

Of course, at the time I didn't realize that this type of planning was a thing! Let's face it, the majority of us have never been taught how to lesson plan.

Which is exactly why we've included this chapter about the EB Lesson Planning Approach. Batch planning, as we've come to call it, is incredibly important. It's *the* cornerstone that we base our entire lesson planning approach on. That's why it's the first aspect we're covering in this chapter.

Here's the basic guiding principle for batch planning: you will sit down at various times throughout the year and plan all of your lessons over a certain period of time.

Batch planning is the *when* of our lesson planning approach. And this can look different for everyone. For example, while I planned for an entire year, we wouldn't necessarily suggest you do that if you're just starting out.

Instead, pick three or four days over the summer leading into the school year, and use those to plan the first few months of school (could be August through October: one day per month, perhaps). Then on a weekend in October, you'll sit down again, uninterrupted, and plan November and December. Over the winter break, you'll do the same thing: pick two days and plan through April. In April, pick two days and plan through the end of the school year.

When we say "plan," all of that is to come later—we'll be discussing planning in detail here shortly.

But batch planning is truly the cornerstone of this lesson planning approach, because it's the only way to ensure that you will no longer work hours upon hours every weekend and school night.

You absolutely *must* batch plan in order to get back all your time outside of teaching. If you don't, you'll never reap the benefits of doing so.

THE RIPPLE EFFECTS OF BATCH PLANNING

[My colleague, Kala Aguado, and I] did not realize what a relief the batch planning was going to bring us for this school year. By having ALL our standards, units, and activities planned for every day, we basically eliminated any added stress in our lives AND we freed up every weeknight and weekend we had for our families.

Not once have we ever felt that we didn't know what to do the next day, week, or month; we no longer have "anxiety Sundays"! It is such a blessing that after a combined 62 years of teaching, we are excited about learning and we feel like it is the first time we actually "get it." We feel like we have been good teachers, but now we have discovered a whole other level to our teaching that we didn't know existed within us. *—Leslie Snyder*

IMPORTANT TIPS TO KEEP IN MIND:

- Your batch planning needs to be *completely* uninterrupted. Turn your phone on airplane mode, lock yourself in a part of your house or go to the local coffee shop, and plan to work for seven or eight hours. Yes, that's a long time, but the rewards that you will see throughout the school year will return to you tenfold.
- If you're just starting out with this concept, plan for just a couple of months at a time. Then set aside one or two days each quarter, trimester, or semester to plan a few more months at a time.
- Over the years, as you get better and better at this, before school even starts in August you'll know exactly what you're teaching on any given day during the school year, because you will have it completely dialed in.
- Your plans *will* change, and that's to be expected. Things come up (assemblies you didn't anticipate, sick days, etc.). Know that you will intentionally plan some wiggle room into your calendar—we'll cover this more in the next section, Scope and Sequence.

SUB PLANS

Expert Tip: While batch planning, don't forget to include two days' worth of sub plans that could work any time throughout your school year.

ACTION ITEM:

Take out your calendar now and block off time when you can batch plan. Literally write it into your planner *right now.* Which days will you plan in the summer, over the winter break, and during the school year?

Scope and Sequence

SCOPE AND SEQUENCE

A scope and sequence is a high-level overview of the units and corresponding standards you are teaching for the entire year or marking period. Think of your scope and sequence as your year-at-a-glance calendar.

The scope and sequence is *where* you write down all of the content you want to cover throughout the school year. It includes every single unit, standard, test, activity, etc., written down in it. Special assemblies, parent-teacher conferences, short days, etc., are also included in your scope and sequence.

This is essentially your road map for the entire year. Once you have it completely filled out, you should be able to pull out your scope and sequence, pick any day, and know exactly what you'll be teaching.

A note here before we continue with this aspect of our lesson planning approach: If you are batch planning in increments throughout the year, your scope and sequence will include only the months you are planning for. So in the summer, you might have planned just through October, and that's completely acceptable (encouraged even, if you're just getting started). But as you master the concept of batch planning more and more, your entire scope and sequence can be completed before school starts in August.

TO GET STARTED WITH YOUR SCOPE AND SEQUENCE, ASK YOURSELF THE FOLLOWING QUESTIONS:

- How many novels (or grammar units, vocabulary units, writing units, etc.) will I be teaching this year?
- How long do I expect each unit to take (or how much time can I allot to each novel/unit)?
- Where do big vacations and important dates fall in the calendar? For example, if report cards are due on a certain day, you'll want to make sure your most recent unit has been completed before then, with time for you to complete any grading for that quarter. Or if spring break is in March rather than April this year, you'll probably want to make sure you've finished the unit before you head off to break, allowing your students (and yourself) time to rest and recharge.

- Where do I want my units to fall in the year? If you're teaching a more challenging topic, you might want to save that for the end of the year, after you've had time to get to know your students and their maturity level has increased. Or if you're teaching writing, you might want to start with the foundation of an essay at the beginning of the year and use that foundational knowledge to build upon through the other writing styles.
- Are there any novels that would be best to teach first, in conjunction with a certain writing style I'll be covering at the same time? For example, if you teach narrative writing at the beginning of the school year, you may also choose to have your students read *The House on Mango Street* at the same time. Personal narratives and Sandra Cisneros's vignettes complement each other so beautifully, it only makes sense to teach them together.

Asking yourself these questions as you look at your scope and sequence allows you to be intentional with your planning. You're not simply starting a unit because you suddenly realized you need another book to teach. A scope and sequence forces you to break that way of thinking.

As you're sitting down to create your scope and sequence, at first you'll be creating a "shell" for your year (or whatever period of time you're planning for). This is the first version of your scope and sequence, your macro-level overview. You're simply organizing where every unit will fall and how all the units fit into your school year.

In the next section of this chapter, you'll be coming back to your scope and sequence again and again as you start adding more layers to it—think: the lessons, assessments, and standards that each day covers.

IMPORTANT TIPS TO KEEP IN MIND:

- Your scope and sequence is meant to be a living, breathing, ever-evolving document. There have been plenty of times where we've had to adjust our scope and sequence because we simply couldn't cover everything we had planned or we had to drop an entire short story unit. That's okay! As time goes on, you'll get better and better at gauging just how much time you'll need for a unit and what is actually feasible in any given year.

- Always, always, always incorporate floating days into your scope and sequence! Floating days are blank days where you have nothing planned. For every unit, we suggest including two floating days. Put them at the end of your unit, so that if something takes longer than you thought, or you have to spend more time reteaching a concept, or you're sick, you'll have those buffer days built into your calendar. This gives you much-needed breathing room with your planning.
- If you teach multiple areas of ELA (vocabulary, grammar, reading, writing, etc.), it is incredibly helpful to create a mini scope and sequence for each area first, and then compile them into one larger, complete scope and sequence. Keep the individual and aggregated versions and adjust them accordingly throughout the year. We've found this simply makes the planning for all areas of ELA more approachable when you sit down to batch plan.

FLOATING DAYS

If you get to the end of your unit and you find that you still have your floating days intact, you've got some options. You can play ELA review games, have an entire reading period, or allow your students a self-selected study day. There are so many options! But it's always better to have the floating days built into your scope and sequence to add flexibility, as opposed to not having them and feeling rushed to cram all your lessons in.

ACTION ITEM

- Create a digital or paper scope and sequence and add in all of the school dates: vacations, holidays, conferences, assemblies. Include every single event that you don't have control over.
- Using the questions two pages ago, start thinking about where you want to add your units into your scope and sequence. If a unit is going to take you about four weeks, add that information. This can look like any of the examples we've included on the following pages from our EB Teachers.

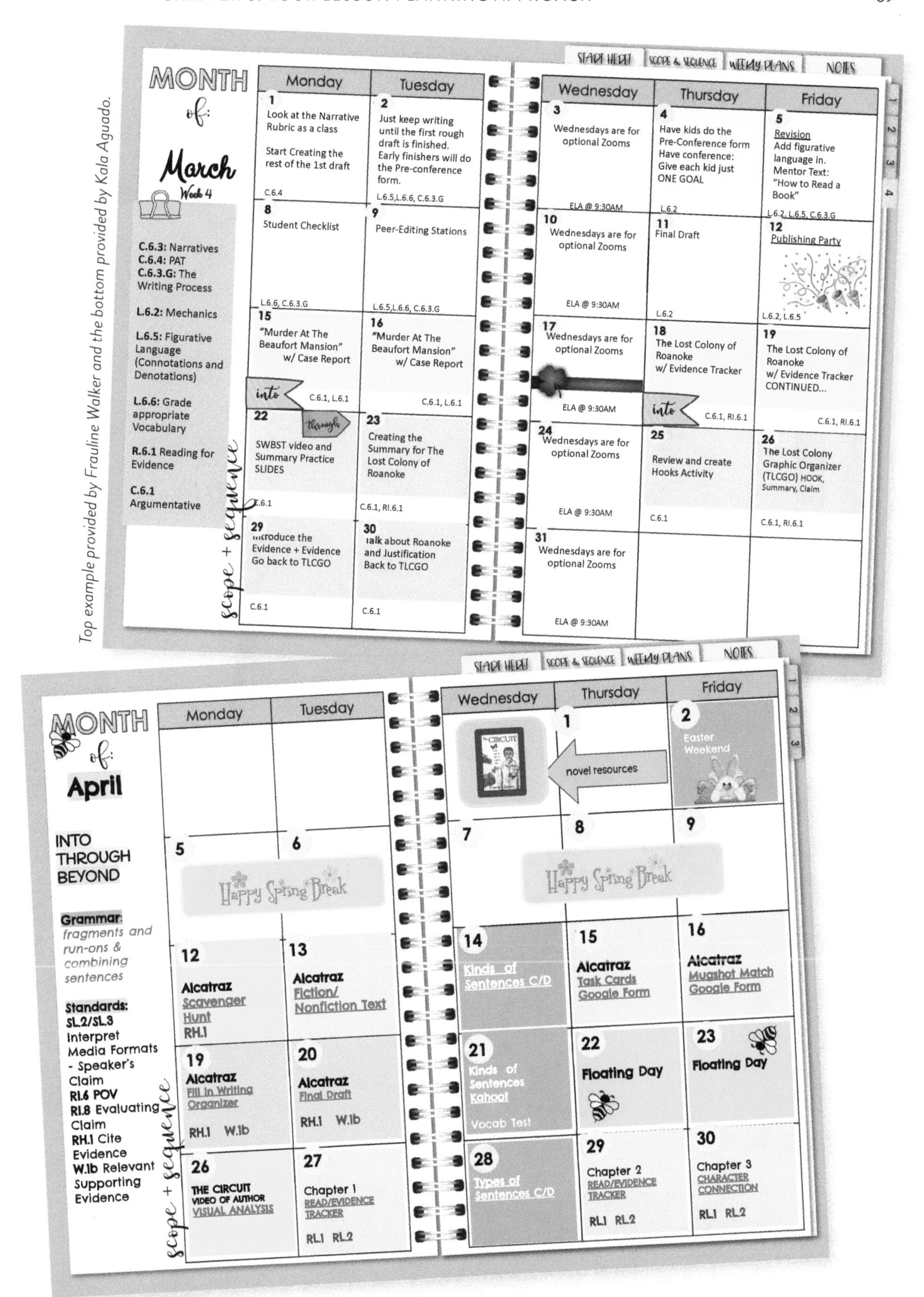

Top example provided by Frauline Walker and the bottom provided by Kala Aguado.

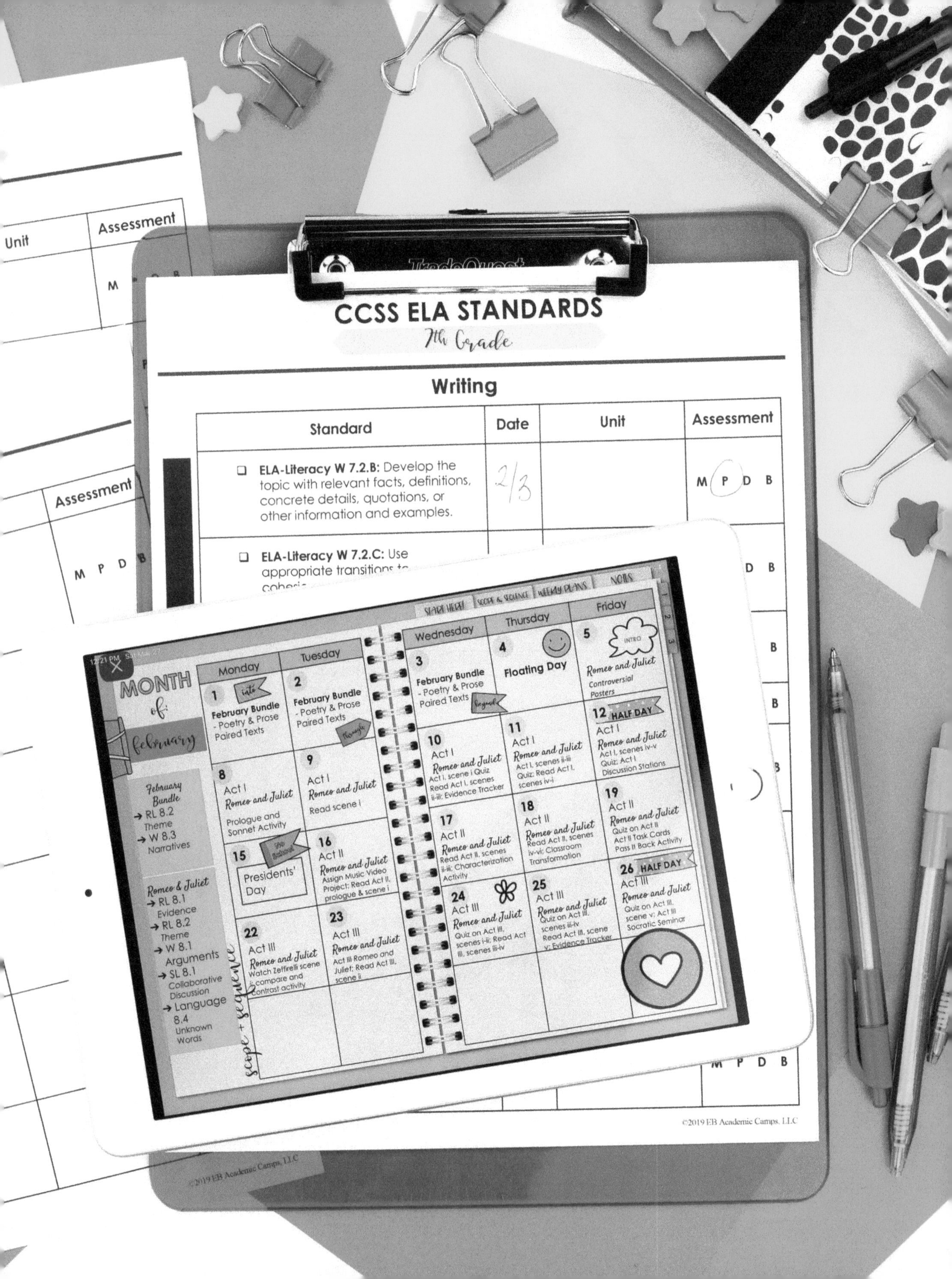
CCSS ELA STANDARDS
7th Grade
Writing
Standard
Date
Unit
Assessment
ELA-Literacy W 7.2.B: Develop the topic with relevant facts, definitions, concrete details, quotations, or other information and examples.
2/3
M P D B
ELA-Literacy W 7.2.C: Use appropriate transitions
©2019 EB Academic Camps, LLC
MONTH of: February
Monday
Tuesday
Wednesday
Thursday
Friday
February Bundle - Poetry & Prose Paired Texts
Floating Day
Romeo and Juliet Controversial Posters
HALF DAY
Presidents' Day
February Bundle
RL 8.2 Theme
W 8.3 Narratives
Romeo & Juliet
RL 8.1 Evidence
RL 8.2 Theme
W 8.1 Arguments
SL 8.1 Collaborative Discussion
Language 8.4 Unknown Words
scope + sequence

Sample provided by Kayla Hanson.

October
SCOPE • SEQUENCE

Kayla Hanson
7th Grade ELA

Monday	Tuesday	Wednesday	Thursday	Friday
			1 • L = Soto Unit cont'd • Evidence Tracker Exercise • G = lesson 2.2	2 • L = Soto Unit cont'd • Finish Evidence Tracker • Vocab. Charades • G = review activity
5 • L = Soto Unit cont'd • Plot Structure • Close Reading • G = additional practice	6 • L = Soto Unit cont'd • Plot Structure Activity cont'd • G = lesson 2.3	7 • L = Soto Unit cont'd • Fig. Language Activity • Close Reading • G = additional practice	8 • L = Soto Unit cont'd • Share Fig. Lang. artwork • Work on Soc. Sem. questions • G = lesson 2.4	9 • L = Soto Unit cont'd • Socratic Seminar • G = review activity
12 • L = Soto Unit cont'd • Grammar Exercise #1/#2	13 • L = Soto Unit cont'd • Grammar Exercise #3 • Intro. to Writing assignment • Review rubric • Begin rough draft	14 • L = Soto Unit cont'd • Continue rough draft • Begin peer editing stations • G = lesson 2.5	15 • L = Soto Unit cont'd • Peer Editing stations • Write final draft • G = test review	16 • L = Soto Unit cont'd • Post assessment • The Dating Game Activity • G = test review
19 • L = Soto Unit cont'd • Begin "The Challenge" • Introduce RTL • G = Ch. 2 posttest	20 • L = Soto Unit cont'd • Close reading • Work on RTL • V = Begin Unit 2	21 • L = Soto Unit cont'd • Evidence Tracker • Work on RTL • G = lesson 3.1	22 • L = Soto Unit cont'd • Work on RTL • V = Unit 2 cont'd	23 END OF Q1 42 DAYS • L = Soto Unit cont'd • Finish RTL • G = lesson 3.2
26 Q2 BEGINS • L = Spooky Short Stories (EB) • G = additional practice	27 • L = Spooky Short Stories (EB) • V = unit 2 cont'd	28 • L = Spooky Short Stories (EB) • G = lesson 3.3	29 • L = Spooky Short Stories (EB) • V = unit 2 cont'd	30 NS: Teacher PD

THE EB TEACHERS' CLUB

The Standards

The next step in our approach to lesson planning is all about the standards. Remember, rigor is one of the three key components of the EB Lesson Planning Approach, so we must use the standards to guide our planning and instruction.

The last thing we want is to be flying blind with no road map! That's something I, Caitlin, can relate to all too well. True confession: My first year teaching high school, I don't think I looked at the standards once, if you can believe it! Not because I was lazy, but because I was so overwhelmed trying to stay caught up with the American literature curriculum I was given. I really didn't know why I was teaching what I was teaching. Sure, students were supposed to learn about Anne Bradstreet and Emily Dickinson, but why? What was I teaching them through those two poets? Other than a love of poetry, I honestly didn't know!

How much more powerful and meaningful it would have been for my students to know the reasoning behind why they were learning what they were learning! Fast-forward to my third year of teaching. After two years of graduate school and *finally* starting to get a grasp on this teaching thing, I realized just how important it was that my students knew *exactly* why we were learning what we were (determining theme and analyzing its development throughout the course of a poem). When I simply told them why, their engagement, their sense of purpose, and their effort skyrocketed!

Plus this made planning much easier for me, because I also realized I didn't have to teach everything on my original scope and sequence. I had been teaching content that didn't cover any of the standards listed for my grade levels—why on earth was I stressing about teaching this content, then? I have to tell you, this was a very freeing moment for me.

We want the same for you. We want you to realize the power behind using the standards as your road map and your guide. They are your compass. Your North Star. The standards are the *why* behind everything that you'll be teaching in your classroom. That's why we wholeheartedly believe in writing our standard-based objectives on the board each day. When our students know what we're trying to accomplish each class period, then it's easier to assess if they're gaining proficiency in that standard.

EXPERT TIP:

Write your standard-based objective on the board before every class period. For example, "Today we will describe how a narrator's or speaker's point of view influences how events are described." This objective is based on the Common Core State Standard for ELA Reading for Literature 5.6. Read the objective aloud with students at the beginning of class, and then at the end of class, spend one minute with your students discussing whether they accomplished that goal or not.

The first thing you want to do is simply read and familiarize yourself with the standards. Start to learn and understand what each of the standards means. Look through the ones you'll need to teach in your grade level. Just by looking at them, you might realize that a particular standard will work really well with a specific novel or short story you're teaching. Allow the standards to spark creativity.

Eventually you'll be plugging the standards into your scope and sequence, but not quite yet—that will come in the final section of this chapter, when you start using the Into, Through, and Beyond Framework in your lesson planning.

As I mentioned earlier when describing my first few years of teaching, one of the best things about using the standards as your guide is that you'll have a clear purpose for teaching what you're teaching, your students will have a clear purpose for learning what they're learning, and you'll also realize you really don't have to teach it *all* (as I used to think). You might find that you're teaching something that isn't even a standard you need to cover! If that's the case, trim the excess and get rid of that lesson or unit. That will make all of the standards you have to cover less daunting and more approachable.

The Into, Through, and Beyond Framework

Now that you know you're going to create your standards-aligned, engaging, and rigorous ELA lessons when you sit down to batch plan your curriculum at predetermined times during the year, let's get into the nitty-gritty of *how* to plan these lessons.

Imagine it's Day One of your scheduled batch planning day. You've found a quiet place to spread out all your materials: scope and sequence, list of inspiring ideas, the texts you plan on using, your grade-level standards, a bag of cheddar Goldfish crackers, and a Coke (maybe that's just us!). You're ready to plan your first unit. You know your students will have to read the text you plan on using and participate in some kind of activities (maybe you don't even know what those are yet), and that the unit will culminate in some kind of assessment . . . perhaps a literary analysis essay or an exam.

> The EB Lesson Planning Approach utilizes a clear road map, or framework, to ensure that the time you set aside to **BATCH PLAN** is used effectively.

Let's be real. It's pretty daunting to stare at those blank dates on your scope and sequence, wanting to create a rigorous and engaging unit but not knowing how to structure it. This is usually when the downward online-lesson-searching spiral begins, and before you know it, you're not even searching lesson plans anymore—you're pinning "easy fall wreaths to make at home" and "dreamy window seat reading nooks."

But what if you looked at those blank dates and asked yourself, *What into, through, and beyond activities do I need to plan?* and you could immediately start penciling in ideas? Wouldn't it be nice to have a clear road map for how to plan so you weren't wasting your time aimlessly searching the internet?

The EB Lesson Planning Approach utilizes a clear road map, or framework, to ensure that the time you set aside to batch plan is used effectively. This framework, which is broken down into "into," "through," and "beyond" lessons, is exactly how we structure all of the lesson plan bundles in our EB Teachers' Club, and it makes the lesson planning portion of our work efficient and enjoyable.

The Into, Through, and Beyond Framework helps you get to the point in planning where you can **CONFIDENTLY** choose from an assortment of lessons you have on hand, tweak them, and use them **AGAIN**.

The Into, Through, and Beyond Framework helps you get to the point in planning where you can confidently choose from an assortment of lessons you have on hand, tweak them, and use them again. Think of it as a recipe of sorts. It's a lot more efficient if you know what meal you're making before you start gathering the ingredients and cooking. Same thing with lesson planning. When you know what type of lesson you need to plan, you can more easily start building one out instead of searching aimlessly online.

Let's break down each component of the Into, Through, and Beyond Framework so you can see the different types of lessons you will be creating to add to your scope and sequence.

We're going to pretend we're planning a short story unit for your middle school ELA class, using Shirley Jackson's "The Lottery," so you can see what the framework looks like in action.

Okay, so we're back at Day One of your scheduled batch planning day. You already know that you're going to teach your short story unit for "The Lottery" in May (in fact, you've penciled that into your scope and sequence) and that you need/want to address the following standards:

Reading for Literature 8.1: Cite the textual evidence that most strongly supports an analysis of what the text says explicitly as well as inferences drawn from the text.

Reading for Literature 8.6: Analyze how differences in the points of view of the characters and the audience or reader (e.g., created through the use of dramatic irony) create such effects as suspense or humor.

Writing 8.1: Write arguments to support claims with clear reasons and relevant evidence.

a. Introduce claim(s), acknowledge and distinguish the claim(s) from alternate or opposing claims, and organize the reasons and evidence logically.
b. Support claim(s) with logical reasoning and relevant evidence, using accurate, credible sources and demonstrating an understanding of the topic or text.
c. Use words, phrases, and clauses to create cohesion and clarify the relationships among claim(s), counterclaims, reasons, and evidence.
d. Establish and maintain a formal style.
e. Provide a concluding statement or section that follows from and supports the argument presented.

Speaking and Listening 8.1: Engage effectively in a range of collaborative discussions (one-on-one, in groups, and teacher-led) with diverse partners on grade 8 topics, texts, and issues, building on others' ideas and expressing their own clearly.

Since all your lessons will be rooted in those standards, you're going to create one "into" lesson, several "through" lessons, and a "beyond" lesson. But what in the world does that look like? Let's define each part of the Into, Through, and Beyond Framework used in the EB Lesson Planning Approach before we return to planning our imaginary unit for "The Lottery."

The "Into"

Think of the "into" part of your unit as the lesson that hooks your students and provides them with any background information necessary for successfully tackling the concepts you'll be covering in your upcoming unit. The "into" lesson is typically one activity or class period. Think of it as the introduction to your unit.

There are tons of engaging "into" lessons you can use in your ELA class that can be repeated throughout the year using different texts and/or ELA topics. Once you have a grab bag of go-to "into" lessons, you can rinse and repeat these activities, saving you hours of planning time. Here are some of our favorites:

- Popcorn Predictions (see page 99)
- Five-Word Wonder (see appendix for the full fill-in-the-blank lesson)
- games (e.g., Connotation Concentration, see page 117)

The "Through"

Immediately following the "into" lesson of a unit, there are typically multiple "through" lessons, where students work through rigorous activities and/or assignments to practice the standards covered in the unit. These might include the following activities:

- annotating a text
- answering text-dependent questions (including justification)
- researching a topic
- prepping for a group project or presentation
- creating a model
- preparing for a mock trial
- participating in a Socratic seminar
- participating in an escape room

The "Beyond"

Think of the "beyond" lesson as your assessment for the unit. This is where students can apply what they have been learning in the previous "through" lessons and extend their thinking.

These might include any of the following activities:

- a response to literature
- a final exam
- a presentation
- a blog post
- a student-created video

Now that you have an overview of the Into, Through, and Beyond Framework used in the EB Lesson Planning Approach, let's return to our short story unit for "The Lottery" and see the framework in action!

Using the Into, Through, and Beyond Framework in an Imaginary Literature Unit

All right, we're back in batch planning mode. We have our ELA standards in front of us, our scope and sequence, a copy of "The Lottery" next to us, and our list of inspiring ideas handy. Now it's time to plan.

We recommend that you start planning your unit with the end in mind, utilizing the concept of backwards planning—that is, planning your "beyond" lesson first. When you know what your students will have to produce for their assessment, then you can more strategically plan the lessons leading up to the assessment, providing key scaffolding that will help set your students up for success.

Start with the "Beyond" Lesson

Recall that the "beyond" lesson is an assessment, an opportunity for students to showcase what they have learned in the "through" lessons. This lesson (like all the others in the Into, Through, and Beyond Framework) should be rooted in the standards. Here is the process for planning the "beyond" lesson:

EXPERT TIP

If you teach your students a consistent writing framework, then you can give them the same essay graphic organizer and rubric any time you have them write a response to literature, ultimately saving you hours and hours of planning time. Merely change the writing prompt each time, and you can rinse and repeat response to literature assignments for your "beyond" lessons in any unit.

STEP ONE

Choose the standard(s) that your assessment will address. For "The Lottery," we like Writing 8.1: "Write arguments to support claims with clear reasons and relevant evidence." This standard and all its substandards (see page 95) lend themselves perfectly to a response to literature (evidence-based essay).

STEP TWO

Now that you know the standard that will be covered and how students will demonstrate mastery of it (response to literature), you must come up with a writing prompt / essential question. Since students, in order to show they have met or exceeded that standard, will have to find logical evidence to support their claim, it's critical that the question you create be text dependent. Here's the question we like to have students answer in their essay for the "beyond" lesson:

> In her short story "The Lottery," Shirley Jackson describes a particularly violent tradition that takes place in a seemingly cordial village. Identify the three most compelling details that Jackson includes in her description that contribute to the reader's shock at the conclusion of the story. Be sure to include evidence from the text to support your reasoning.

STEP THREE

Pencil the "beyond" lesson onto your scope and sequence. Estimate how many class periods this lesson might take. If you are teaching 8th graders and this lesson is being done at the end of the year, it may be reasonable to expect students to complete an in-class, text-dependent essay in one class period. If you are teaching 6th graders who struggle with writing, this same "beyond" lesson may take two class periods: one to review the writing prompt and for students to outline their evidence, and another for them to write the essay. (Keep in mind that the more you use the EB Lesson Planning Approach, the better you will become at gauging how long a particular lesson may take.)

STEP FOUR

Prep any handouts or other materials needed for this lesson. Create an essay graphic organizer and a rubric aligned to the writing standard on which your lesson focuses. File these materials away to be used on the future date of the "beyond" lesson for "The Lottery."

Create Your "Into" Lesson

Once you have your "beyond" lesson penciled into your scope and sequence, you're ready to create your "into" lesson. Recall that an "into" lesson is meant to hook your students and provide them with any background knowledge you deem necessary for the unit.

Here's the process for planning your "into" lesson:

STEP ONE

Choose the standard(s) that your "into" lesson will address. For "The Lottery," we like Speaking and Listening 8.1: "Engage effectively in a range of collaborative discussions (one-on-one, in groups, and teacher-led) with diverse partners on grade 8 topics, texts, and issues, building on others' ideas and expressing their own clearly."

STEP TWO

Refer to your list of inspiring ideas and choose an engaging activity that aligns with the standard(s) you selected. For "The Lottery," we like to use one of our favorite "into" lessons, Popcorn Predictions. This engaging activity makes an effective "into" lesson because predicting encourages students to not only think strategically but also ask relevant questions. It allows them to better understand the text and make thoughtful connections to what they read, and it can improve reading comprehension. Plus it's a fun activity that has them practicing a key speaking and listening standard. Win-win!

This activity is meant to get students up and moving around the room, "popping" from one student to the next as they collaborate to create predictions about the story. Each student is given a strip of paper with one or two sentences from the story written on it. Students carefully read their sentence(s) and then move around the room to make connections with other students. When they meet a classmate, they read their strip of paper aloud and make a prediction about the story. Once they have made a prediction, both students move on to other classmates and repeat the

EXPERT TIP

Create a generic Popcorn Predictions graphic organizer that can be used each time you have your students participate in this activity for different pieces of literature. As students "pop" around the room sharing their sentence strips with classmates, they can write down various predictions and monitor how their predictions change as new information is accumulated. You can simply make a bunch of copies of the graphic organizer in advance and have them ready to go for multiple "into" lessons during the year. Talk about a time-saver!

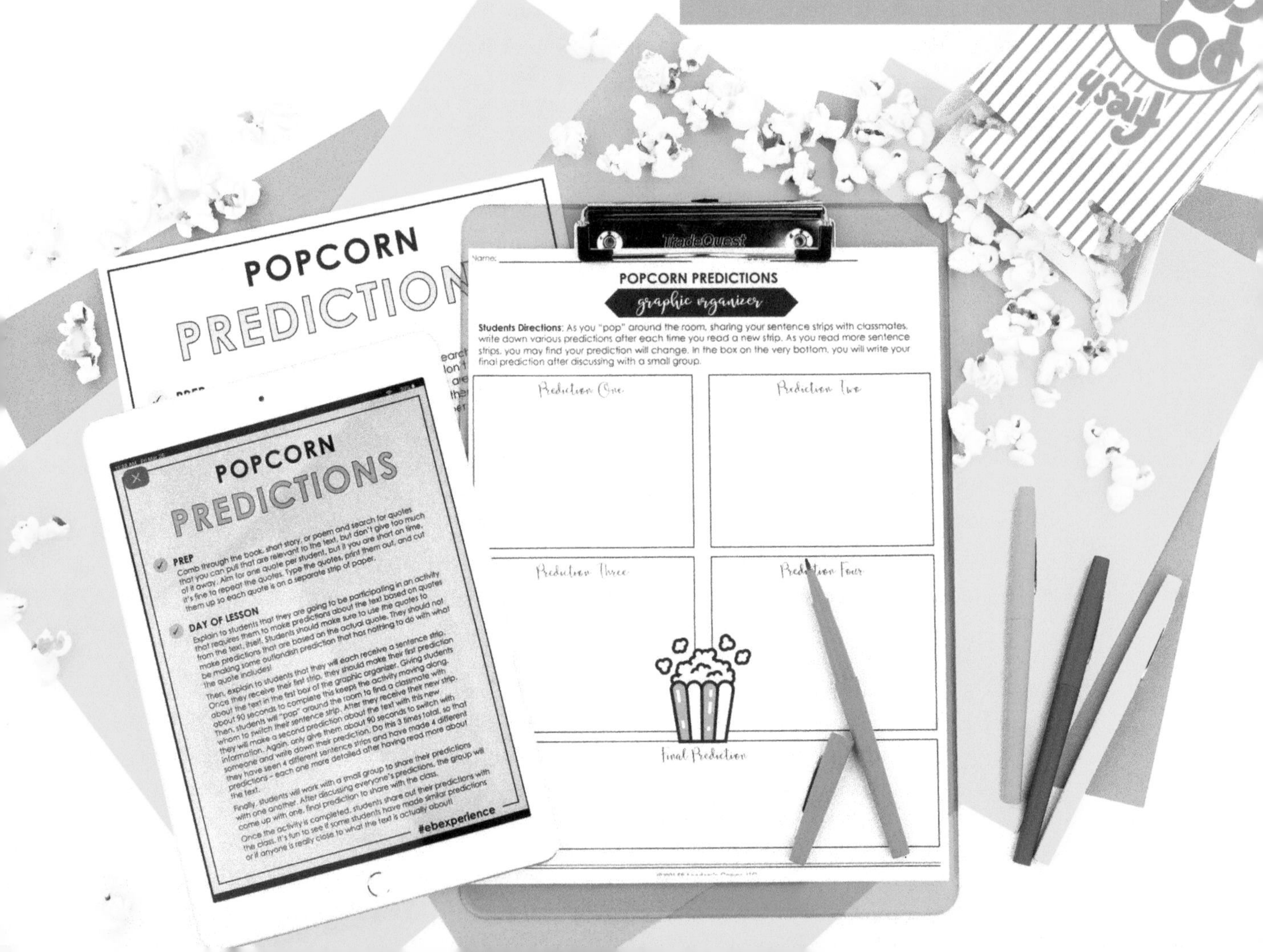

process. Each prediction may become more elaborate as students build on past sentence strips they have heard from previous classmates. Finally, students can form small groups to compose one agreed-upon prediction for the story to share with the class.

STEP THREE

Pencil the "into" lesson into your scope and sequence. Since Popcorn Predictions is a quick activity, it shouldn't take longer than one class period.

STEP FOUR

Now that you know you will be using Popcorn Predictions for your "into" lesson, prep any necessary materials. Create a document with interesting sentences from the text, in this case "The Lottery." Make sure that the sentences allow room for interpretation but don't give away information that will ruin the outcome of the story.

Map Out Your "Through" Lessons

Since you have already created your "into" and "beyond" lessons, you have essentially bookended your short story unit. Now, it's time to plan the "through" lessons that will get students practicing the standards as they continue to interact with the text. These lessons should all be planned with the end goal in mind (whatever students will be doing in the "beyond" lesson—in this case writing a response to literature). As you plan this imaginary unit for "The Lottery," ask yourself what skills your students need to practice in order to confidently and successfully compose a response to literature for the prompt you created.

Well, if students are writing a text-dependent essay about the three most compelling details in Jackson's story that contribute to the reader's shock at its conclusion, then they must have practice finding evidence from the text as well as experience analyzing any details in the story that may contribute to the reader's shock. So the "through" lessons must address these concepts.

Here's the process for planning your "through" lesson(s). (Keep in mind that it may take multiple class periods to provide students with the lessons necessary to successfully complete their assignment in the "beyond" lesson. For example, if you were planning a novel unit instead of an imaginary short story unit, your "through" lessons may take weeks and include actually reading the novel!)

STEP ONE

Choose the standard(s) that your "through" lessons will address. Again, the lessons students complete in this phase should ideally be scaffolding for their "beyond" lesson. Each lesson you plan may cover one particular standard or address multiple standards. For "The Lottery," standards Reading for Literature 8.1 (Cite the textual evidence that most strongly supports an analysis of what the text says explicitly as well as inferences drawn from the text) and Reading for Literature 8.6 (Analyze how differences in the points of view of the characters and the audience or reader [e.g., created through the use of dramatic irony] create such effects as suspense or humor) both provide scaffolding opportunities for students before they write their response to literature in the "beyond" lesson.

STEP TWO

Start planning multiple lessons that support students' mastery of these standards. Since you already have your writing prompt / essential question created for students' response to literature, align your lessons around the question. For example, one of your "through" lessons will be to read and annotate "The Lottery." As you read, you could have students note instances of foreshadowing and suspense. This will come in handy when they write their response to literature and need to include evidence from the text showing how the author described details that lead to the reader's ultimate shock at the conclusion of the story.

The other standard chosen for this unit focuses on the characters' points of view, so some kind of character-driven activity makes complete sense as another "through" lesson. We like to have students imagine they are participating in an interview with two central characters in the story, Mrs. Hutchinson and Mr. Summers. We provide students with open-ended critical-thinking questions (e.g., "Does the lottery tradition ever alienate members of your community? Explain.") and have them formulate responses as if they are answering from the perspective of those characters. Students can support their inferred answers with evidence from the text, further preparing them to write their text-dependent essay as they practice finding relevant evidence.

> **EXPERT TIP**
>
> Recall that when you are building out your scope and sequence, we suggest leaving two to three floating days per unit in case you need to move lessons around due to an unexpected assembly or a lesson taking longer than expected. If this is your first time using the EB Lesson Planning Approach and you're not sure how long each lesson will take, you may even wish to leave an extra floating day or two.

STEP THREE

Pencil the "through" lessons into your scope and sequence.

STEP FOUR

Prep any handouts or other materials needed for all "through" lessons.

Here are two examples of "through" lessons we use in our short story unit for "The Lottery."

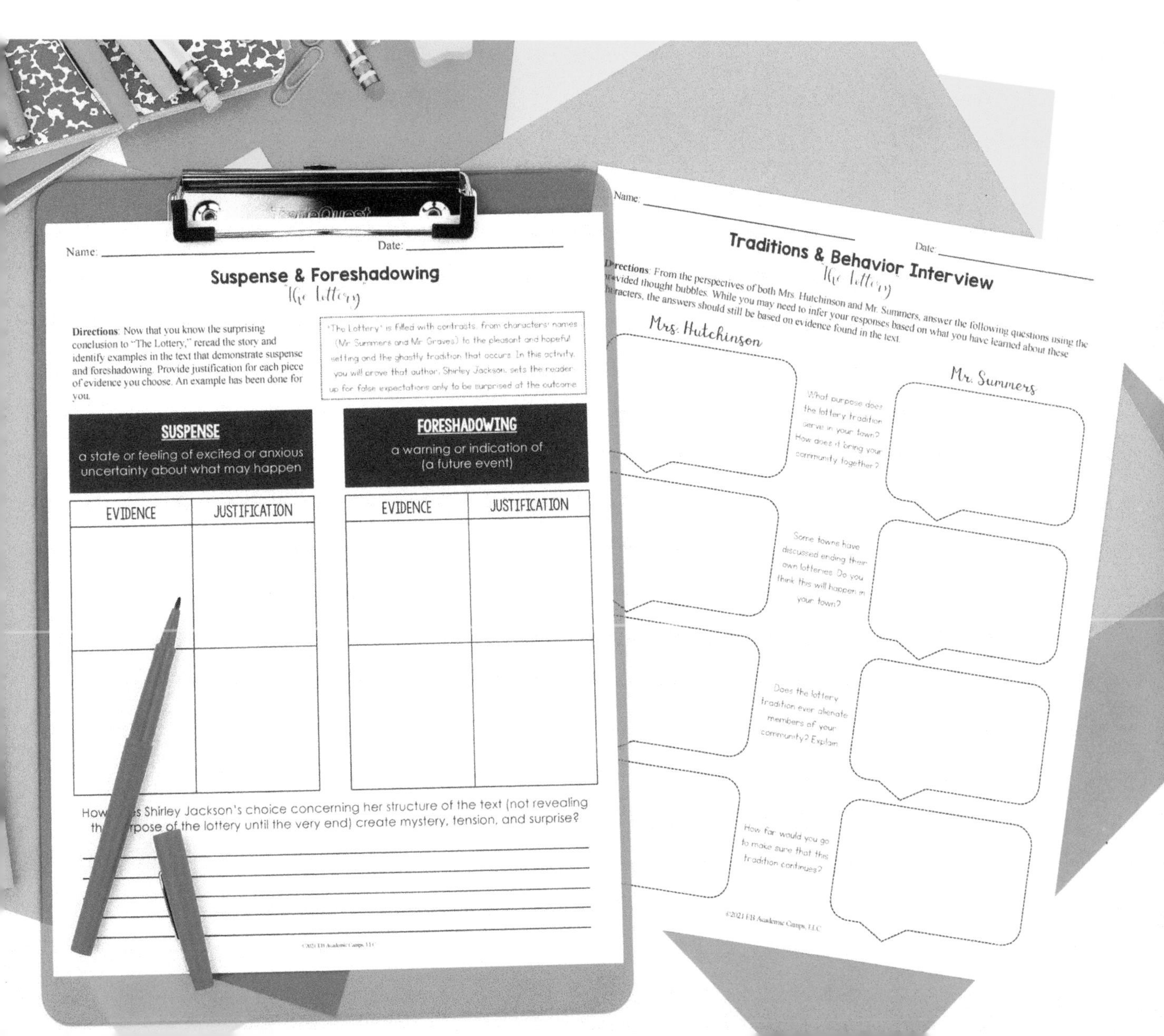

Rinse, Repeat, and Celebrate!

Whew! We've successfully planned one short story unit using the Into, Through, Beyond Framework. But this is just one of many units that need to be planned for the year (or month or semester). Now what? You're going to rinse and repeat. Take a quick break from batch planning, have a snack, and then dive back in. Choose your next piece of literature or ELA topic, find the standards you need to cover, refer to your list of inspiring ideas, start figuring out your "into," "through," and "beyond" lessons, and pencil them into your scope and sequence.

IMPORTANT TIPS TO KEEP IN MIND

- When choosing the order of your units, keep in mind the complexity of the texts your students will be reading and the tasks involved. One unit might be better suited for May, when students are more proficient at the various standards, while another unit would work better at the beginning of the year, when these new grade-level standards are being introduced. For example, we might teach *The House on Mango Street* at the beginning of the year in 8th grade, because it's a shorter text that covers themes of personal growth and self-discovery—a very appropriate unit as we get to know our students.
- Remember, because you're planning each unit with the end in mind, you'll want to begin your lesson plans with your assessment. Will it be an essay, a test, a project, or something else? Once you decide that, you can start planning activities and lessons that will set students up for success for that assessment.
- Keep your eyes on the prize. By dedicating a set time to implement the EB Lesson Planning Approach, you will walk away with detailed, rigorous, and engaging lessons for the next few weeks or even months! Each time you use the EB Lesson Planning Approach, you'll become more efficient and the process will get easier.

ACTION ITEM:

- Take a minute to jot down some ideas that you could potentially use for an "into," "through," or "beyond" lesson for any literature unit you currently teach.

Chapter 6:

STEPPING INTO YOUR ROLE OF EMPOWERED EDUCATOR

I, JESSICA, FELT at the top of my game and my absolute best as a teacher during my four years as the 5th grade teacher at my school in LA. Not only did I adore my students and their families and become close friends with my coworkers, but I also was truly excited to teach each morning. I was confident that the lessons I had prepared in advance were rigorous and engaging.

I was reminded of this time in my teaching career just the other day, when I stumbled upon the private 5th grade Facebook group I created for my students years ago. I had not visited this group since 2010, but I clicked on it. I was immediately transported back to my class that year—now sophomores in college!—as I looked through pictures of their Pumpkin Explorers Project and photos from our field trip to Griffith Observatory. I read through some of their chapter 5 blog post responses for *Bud, Not Buddy.* And then I read their daily posts. Each day, it was a student's job to post something about what they had learned, so that their parents had a good grasp of what was happening in our classroom. It was so fun to see what my students chose to write about. Here is one student's post:

> "Today in English, we performed our skits in front of the class. Then in P.E we played kickball. It was fun! In math, we learned how to multiply fractions and played games. During recess, the office rang the bell, but it was a false alarm, so we got 5 more minutes of recess. Then, we wrote stories from the point of view (P.O.V.) of Winnie and Jesse in *Tuck Everlasting.* Then we read *City of Ember.* It was so cool in 5th grade today. :)"
>
> —Janessa

Reading it, I specifically remembered the point of view stories that Janessa referenced. We were about to wrap up our literature unit for *Tuck Everlasting,* and students were writing stories from the perspective of either Winnie or Jesse, two central characters in the novel. Students who wrote from Jesse's POV were trying to convince Winnie to drink the magical water that would allow her to live forever with him. Students had to use evidence from the text and justification within their story to support Jesse's perspective.

The students who were writing from Winnie's perspective could either choose or decline the water, again citing evidence from the text and supporting their choice with justification. Then they all sat in the front of the classroom—the students who had written from Jesse's POV facing those who had written from Winnie's POV—and took turns reading their stories. After each "Jesse" story was read, a student with a "Winnie" story responded and we could see if Winnie chose to drink the water.

Reading Janessa's snippet from what we did in 5th grade on October 21, 2010, made me smile, recalling how much fun we had as students proudly shared their stories during literature class. It was the kind of fun where they didn't realize they were actually doing work. Looking back on that memory makes my teacher heart happy.

Those four years in my teaching career, my last four years in a self-contained classroom—I switched to part-time when I started having my own children—were when I truly stepped into the role of an empowered ELA teacher.

Getting Started

We hope that at this point you're excited to start implementing the EB Lesson Planning Approach into your daily teaching life. You're ready to step into the role of an empowered ELA teacher!

To help you get the fastest results in the shortest amount of time, we've laid out every step succinctly here, in this final chapter of the book. While each chapter goes in-depth with the three components of the EB Lesson Planning Approach (engagement, rigor, and planning), this chapter will break it down for you in simple steps.

You've learned a lot throughout this book, and while each component of the EB Lesson Planning Approach is independently important to the process of becoming an empowered educator, the beauty happens when all three components work together and complement each other in your classroom.

We suggest you implement them in your planning in the following order: your lesson planning approach, engagement, then rigor.

We recommend starting with the lesson planning approach because this will get you moving quickly toward being that empowered ELA teacher you are going to become. You'll need to set aside time to work through the four aspects of lesson planning: batch planning; your scope and sequence; the standards; and the Into, Through, and Beyond Framework.

Once you've created the foundation for your curriculum with your lesson planning, you can add the engagement piece into the Into, Through, and Beyond Framework you'll be utilizing from now on. Finally, the rigor component is where you'll take your lessons to the next level, continuously pushing your students toward their highest potential.

How to Ensure You *Stay* an Empowered ELA Teacher

Once you've made the commitment to sit down and plan using our EB Lesson Planning Approach, you'll want to make sure you stay in your new role of an empowered ELA teacher. There's nothing quite like teaching from this state of being, and you'll want to do everything you can to stay here. So we've put together some suggestions to help you hold yourself accountable *and* take your role to new heights.

Continually Switch Things Up

When we reach the top of our game, it can be difficult to stay there or feel challenged to push ourselves even further. Clearly you want to be the best you can possibly be; otherwise you wouldn't have made it this far!

We suggest you teach and plan from a state where you continue to switch things up and add fresh activities to your existing units. Think about the topics, texts, and essential questions you want to cover or change for the following year. Ask your students what they did or didn't like throughout your year together. Taking their feedback into account, ask yourself if there is a lesson or unit you could improve upon. Or if there's one lesson your students loved, ask yourself how you could take the things they enjoyed about that lesson and incorporate them into other lessons throughout the year.

As an empowered ELA teacher, you will naturally continue to research new texts, topics, and approaches to teaching your lessons. Think of yourself as being like an athlete who is constantly practicing their skill and talent. You will consistently be honing your own skills and talents as an educator, and this allows you to stay at the top of your game.

Make It a Habit to Know Your Numbers

Know your data! We love this one, because looking at your students' past test scores to see what standards or general topics they struggled with last year tells you exactly where your focus should be now. How empowering is that?

By knowing where your students are at any given moment, including the moment they walk into your classroom, you're able to adjust your instruction based precisely on their needs. (Remember how we said a scope and sequence is a living, breathing document that is created to be flexible?) You might find that you're not able to dive directly into counterclaims in argumentative writing because your data shows that your students struggled with simply identifying claims.

By making it a habit to know your numbers (your students' data), you'll be prepared for the gaps in your students' understanding of concepts that you'll be covering throughout the year. If you don't know your numbers, you won't be able to fill those gaps!

This is especially important when you batch plan later in the year, after you've worked with your students for a few months. You'll be able to plan accordingly, in a way that meets your students exactly where they are. That's a pretty powerful place to be as an educator.

Utilize Repetition to Find Even More Balance in Your Life

If you adopt, fully buy into, and play to win using the EB Lesson Planning Approach, you are guaranteeing that you will find balance in your life. But what if we told you that you could simply use a bit of repetition to find *even more* of that elusive balance?

It really is quite simple. We suggest you use repetition whenever possible, so lesson planning doesn't take days upon days to complete. Repetition is inherent to the Into, Through, and Beyond Framework because you'll be creating continuity in your lessons. Using this framework also helps you determine what kind of activity or lesson you need to plan. You'll no longer be sitting there scratching your head, wondering what on earth you're supposed to be teaching.

Instead you'll plug your lessons into the "into," the "through," or the "beyond." And here's where the magic happens. Once you've created certain activities for each part of the framework, you can simply rinse and repeat. Yes! Use the same activities or lessons again for a different novel or unit. You are allowed, even encouraged, to do this.

For instance, if your students love using Popcorn Predictions in class, do it again! Or if you've found great success with Socratic seminars, plan one or two for every unit you'll be covering throughout the year. Were your students completely engrossed in the investigation trial you used at the beginning of the year? Simply use the same concept again for another unit.

Look at repetition as a small key to adding more balance into your life.

Keep Using the EB Lesson Planning Approach

We know that once you start using this approach to lesson planning, your entire world as a teacher will completely change.

Remember that frazzled and overwhelmed teacher that we spoke about at the beginning of the book? The one who was just barely making it through each day? It's time to completely say goodbye to that teacher, because this is the moment when you make the commitment, fully, to yourself and to the EB Lesson Planning Approach.

You are about to become the empowered ELA teacher.

The teacher who is inspired, confident, and prepared each day. The teacher whose ELA lessons are rigorous and engaging, allowing students to master the standards while discovering the joy of learning. The teacher who no longer sacrifices nights and weekends to prep lessons each week, having planned in advance in order to find balance between school and personal life.

This picture of teaching can be achieved. It is simply a matter of implementing the approach we've laid out for you.

It's time to *Thrive.*

Appendix:

LESSON PLAN MATERIALS

LESSON PLAN MATERIALS

Name ______________________ Date ____________

Socratic Seminar

observation checklist

Student Directions: During the Socratic Seminar, tally how many times your partner participates. Put your tally marks in the appropriate box based on what kind of participation your partner engages in. After the Socratic Seminar has ended, answer the questions.

POSITIVE PARTICIPATION	AREAS FOR IMPROVEMENT
• Speaks in the discussion	• Interrupts another student
• References evidence from the text	• Participates in side conversation
• Asks a follow-up question	• Doesn't allow others to speak

REFLECTION QUESTIONS

1. What was the strongest piece of evidence your partner used? Why?

2. When did your partner elaborate on a classmate's point instead of just sharing their own information?

3. What would YOU like to have contributed to the conversation but didn't have the chance to?

Socratic Seminar Rubric

Student Name ____________________

Circle the description that best applies to today's Socratic Seminar.

How often did the student participate?	Always	Often	Seldom	Never
Did the student share comments voluntarily, or did they need to be prompted?	Always participated without needing o be prompted	Often participated without needing to be prompted	Only participated with prompting from the teacher or leader	Never participated
How would you describe the student's analysis of the text?	Excellent; the student made thoughtful connections and inferences	Average; the student made general connections or comments that were sometimes disconnected	Weak; the student did not analyze the text but simply summarized, or the student's comments were completely disconnected	Difficult to know due to lack of participation
How would you describe the student's understanding of the text?	Excellent; the student clearly grasped the main ideas and the author's point of view	Average; the student vaguely referred to main ideas in the text, but could not cite specifics	Weak; the student mixed up details or main ideas from the text	Difficult to know due to lack of participation
How did the student exhibit active listening? (Circle all that apply.)	Eye contact with the speaker was apparent	Nodded in agreement with the speaker	Commented on a classmate's analysis and moved the discussion along	Asked questions relevant to the discussion
Did the student use evidence from the text to support their analysis?	Always	Often	Seldom (said their opinion more than evidence)	Never (only said their opinion)

Connotation + Denotation

Connotation Concentration

instructions for use

This lesson has students participating in a game of Connotation Concentration. You can make multiple copies of the game and have sets of partners playing at the same time, or it can be used as a center activity.

This game requires students to identify and match examples of connotative language. It's an important warm up, as later in the unit, students will be analyzing connotative language in a given text and its impact on the text's tone.

1. Review the difference between connotation and denotation using the **Connotation and Denotation Posters.**
   - On the first day of this unit, hang the posters prominently in your classroom. You will refer to them as you introduce the concepts of denotations and connotations. We highly suggest displaying the posters throughout the entire unit.
   - Review the difference between connotation and denotation using the posters provided. Explain to your students that words can have quite similar denotations (definitions) as seen in the examples provided on the poster ("group," "club," "clique") but quite different connotations. *Note: the definitions used to illustrate this example are groups at their most basic level: a collection of people. Yet, their connotations vary from positive to neutral to negative.*
2. Distribute the **Word Chart Handout** to students and work together to determine words that might fit in each row.
3. Explain that students will be playing a game called **Connotation Concentration** to practice finding pairs of words that, although they have similar denotations, have different connotations.
4. Determine how you will use this game (center, whole-class playing at the same time, etc.), and make copies of the **Connotation Concentration Game Cards** and the **Connotation Concentration Game Rules Handout** accordingly.
5. Distribute one set of cards to each pair of students.
6. Pairs of students will practice identifying words with similar denotations and related connotations (e.g., "group," "club," "clique"). Each time they find a match, they get to keep that set of cards. Students will follow the instructions on the **Game Rules Handout**.
7. A **Connotation Concentration Answer Key** has been provided for you as well.

DENOTATION

THE *literal* MEANING OF A WORD

Group: a set of more than one person
Club: a set of more than one person
Clique: a set of more than one person

CONNOTATION

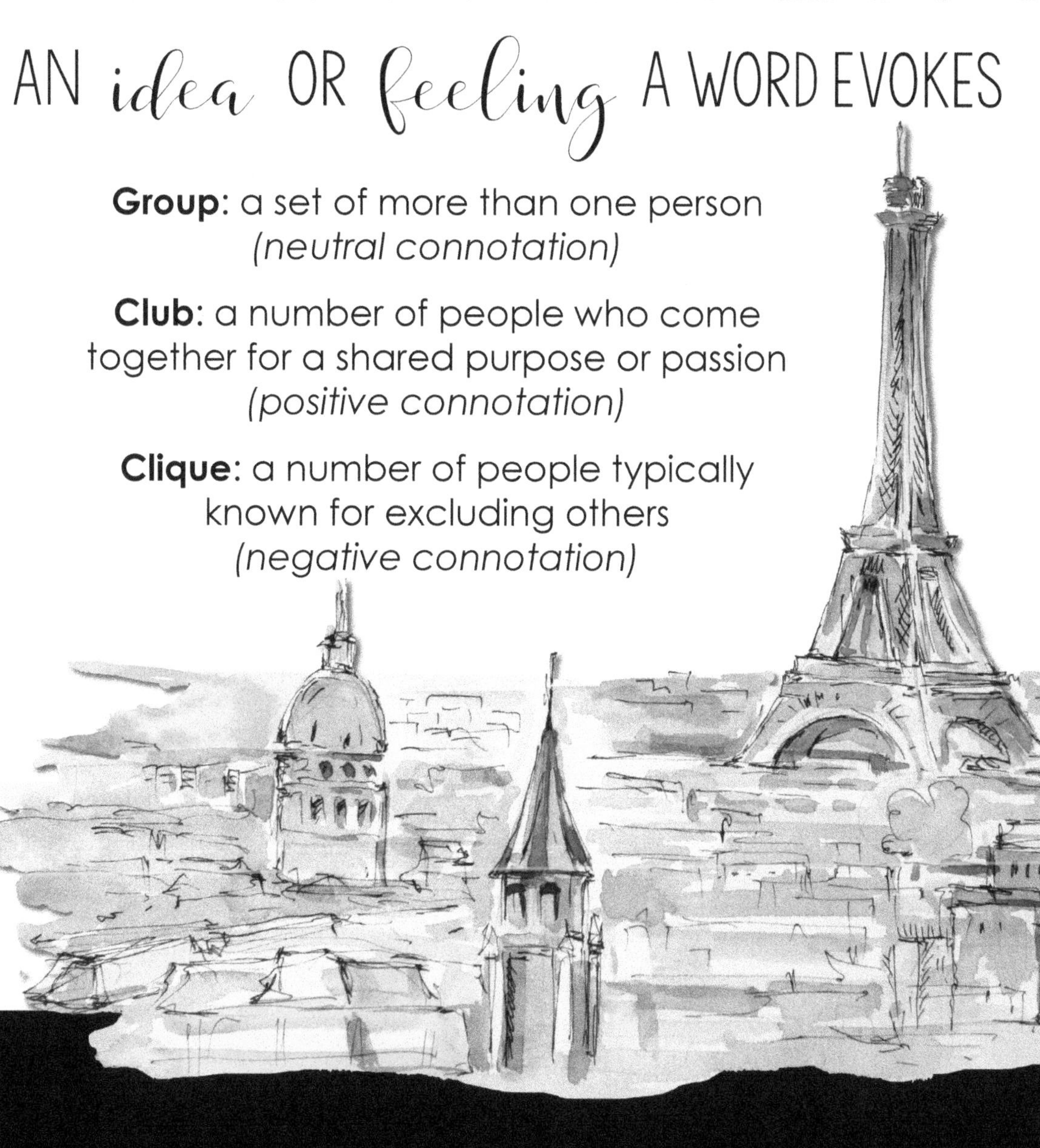
AN idea OR feeling A WORD EVOKES
Group: a set of more than one person
(neutral connotation)
Club: a number of people who come together for a shared purpose or passion
(positive connotation)
Clique: a number of people typically known for excluding others
(negative connotation)

Name: ____________________ Date: ____________________

CONNOTATIONS

word chart

Student Directions: In the middle column of the chart below, you will find seven words with neutral connotations. Complete each row by finding a word with the same denotation but a positive connotation, and a word with the same denotation but a negative connotation. You may need to reference a dictionary or thesaurus to help you with this.

POSITIVE CONNOTATION	NEUTRAL CONNOTATION	NEGATIVE CONNOTATION
	saving	
	tenacious	
	confident	
	different	
	selective	
	old	
	happy	

ANSWER KEY

CONNOTATIONS

word chart

Student Directions: In the middle column of the chart below, you will find seven words with neutral connotations. Complete each row by finding a word with the same denotation but a positive connotation, and a word with the same denotation but a negative connotation. You may need to reference a dictionary or thesaurus to help you with this.

POSITIVE CONNOTATION	NEUTRAL CONNOTATION	NEGATIVE CONNOTATION
thrifty	saving	cheap
steadfast	tenacious	stubborn
courageous	confident	self-centered
unique	different	strange
meticulous	selective	picky
vintage	old	dilapidated
elated	happy	manic

CHILDLIKE	YOUTHFUL	IMMATURE
JUVENILE	RELAXED	LAID-BACK
LACKADAISICAL	EASYGOING	SLIM
SLENDER	SKINNY	THIN
CHEAP	FRUGAL	MISERLY

ECONOMICAL	STEADFAST	TENACIOUS
STUBBORN	OBSTINATE	INQUISITIVE
INTERESTED	CURIOUS	PRYING
STENCH	SMELL	AROMA
SCENT	METICULOUS	SELECTIVE

PICKY	DISCERNING	VINTAGE
OLD	AGED	DECREPIT
CHATTY	TALKATIVE	MOTORMOUTH
CONVERSATIONAL	CONFIDENT	EGOTISTICAL
SECURE	PROUD	ELATED

HAPPY	CONTENT	MANIC
WEALTHY	AFFLUENT	RICH
PRIVILEGED		

CONNOTATION CONCENTRATION
directions

<u>Number of Players</u>: 2

<u>Materials</u>:
Set of 52 matching cards

<u>Strategy</u>:
One good strategy to use with Connotation Concentration is not to always turn over the card you are sure of first. For example, if you *know exactly* where a certain word is, but only *think* you know where a matching word is, turn over the guess first.

<u>Starting the Game</u>:
To set up Connotation Concentration, first shuffle the cards well and then place each card face down in 4 rows of 13 cards each.

<u>Taking a Turn</u>:
Each player takes a turn by turning two cards over. If the cards have similar denotations and related connotations (e.g., childlike, youthful), then the player picks up the cards and keeps them. If the cards don't have similar connotations, the player turns the cards back over. If the player gets a match, they get to go again until they fail to get a match.

The game is over when all of the cards have been matched and picked up.

<u>Winning the Game</u>:
The winner of the game is the player with the most matches once all the cards have been picked up.

<u>Alternative Way to Play</u>:
You can play Connotation Concentration by yourself and then time yourself to try and complete the game faster each round. You can also try to finish the game in fewer and fewer turns.

CONNOTATION CONCENTRATION
directions

Number of Players: 2

Materials:
Set of 52 matching cards

Strategy:
One good strategy to use with Connotation Concentration is not to always turn over the card you are sure of first. For example, if you know exactly where a certain word is, but only think you know where a matching word is, turn over the guess first.

Starting the Game:
To set up Connotation Concentration, first shuffle the cards well and then place each card face down in 4 rows of 13 cards each.

Taking a Turn:
Each player takes a turn by turning two cards over. If the cards have similar denotations and related connotations (e.g., childlike, youthful), then the player picks up the cards and keeps them. If the cards don't have similar connotations, the player turns the cards back over. If the player gets a match, they get to go again until they fail to get a match.

The game is over when all of the cards have been matched and picked up.

Winning the Game:
The winner of the game is the player with the most matches once all the cards have been picked up.

Alternative Way to Play:
You can play Connotation Concentration by yourself and then time yourself to try and complete the game faster each round. You can also try to finish the game in fewer and fewer turns.

©2021 EB Academic Camps, LLC

CONNOTATION CONCENTRATION

answer key

• childlike • youthful • immature • juvenile	• relaxed • laid-back • lackadaisical • easygoing
• slim • slender • skinny • thin	• cheap • frugal • miserly • economical
• steadfast • tenacious • stubborn • obstinate	• inquisitive • interested • curious • prying
• stench • smell • aroma • scent	• meticulous • selective • picky • discerning
• vintage • old • aged • decrepit	• chatty • talkative • motormouth • conversational
• confident • egotistical • secure • proud	• elated • happy • content • manic
• wealthy • affluent • rich • privileged	

Pronoun! Card Game

student directions

1. Choose a dealer to shuffle and deal five cards to each player.
2. Place the remaining cards in the middle (face down in a stack) and flip one card up and lay it to the right of the stack.
3. The player to the left of the dealer begins the game. The player reads the sentence on the bottom of the card.
4. The player may then lay a card down from their hand that matches the color, shape, and type of pronoun that is used in the sentence written on the card. For example, if the card lying face up contains a subjective pronoun in the sentence, the player should lay down a card that says "subjective" on it, OR they may also play a "WILD" card or an action card (Draw Two, Reverse, Skip) that matches the color card that is face up.
5. The player must read the sentence on the card and share which type of pronoun is being portrayed (even if they choose to use a "Wild" or action card). If the other players agree, then the player can lay down their card and play continues to the left. (If players are unsure, the teacher has an answer key to help).
6. If the other students disagree with the player's answer, the player may not lay down a card, and instead must draw two additional cards.
7. If a player does not have a card to play (none of their cards match the color or type of pronoun), they must draw one card from the stacked pile. If they can play that card, they may. If not, the game continues with the next player on the left.
8. If players run out of cards to draw from, simply shuffle the cards from the discard pile and continue playing.
9. The game continues until a player has only one card left. That player must call out, "Pronoun!" before someone notices. If the player forgets and another player notices, the player with only one card must draw two additional cards from the "draw" pile.
10. The game is over when a player gets rid of all their cards.

Pronoun! Card Game

student directions

1. Choose a dealer to shuffle and deal five cards to each player.
2. Place the remaining cards in the middle (face down in a stack) and flip one card up and lay it to the right of the stack.
3. The player to the left of the dealer begins the game. The player reads the sentence on the bottom of the card.
4. The player may then lay a card down from their hand that matches the color, shape, and type of pronoun that is used in the sentence written on the card. For example, if the card lying face up contains a subjective pronoun in the sentence, the player should lay down a card that says "subjective" on it, OR they may also play a "WILD" card or an action card (Draw Two, Reverse, Skip) that matches the color card that is face up.
5. The player must read the sentence on the card and share which type of pronoun is being portrayed (even if they choose to use a "Wild" or action card). If the other players agree, then the player can lay down their card and play continues to the left. (If players are unsure, the teacher has an answer key to help).
6. If the other students disagree with the player's answer, the player may not lay down a card, and instead must draw two additional cards.
7. If a player does not have a card to play (none of their cards match the color or type of pronoun), they must draw one card from the stacked pile. If they can play that card, they may. If not, the game continues with the next player on the left.
8. If players run out of cards to draw from, simply shuffle the cards from the discard pile and continue playing.
9. The game continues until a player has only one card left. That player must call out, "Pronoun!" before someone notices. If the player forgets and another player notices, the player with only one card must draw two additional cards from the "draw" pile.
10. The game is over when a player gets rid of all their cards.

©2021 EB Academic Camps, LLC

PRONOUN!

PRONOUN!

PRONOUN!

PRONOUN!

PRONOUN!

PRONOUN!

OBJECTIVE

Identify the proper case for the pronoun.

I love anchovies on pizza.

OBJECTIVE

Identify the proper case for the pronoun.

You aren't going to wear that, right?

SUBJECTIVE

Identify the proper case for the pronoun.

Mario doesn't understand why he can't go.

DRAW TWO!

Identify the proper case for the pronoun.

That's fine with me.

SKIP!

Identify the proper case for the pronoun.

This is mine, so don't wreck it.

REVERSE!

Identify the proper case for the pronoun.

Ask Leticia to drive in her car.

PRONOUN!

PRONOUN!

PRONOUN!

PRONOUN!

PRONOUN!

PRONOUN!

POSSESSIVE

Identify the proper case for the pronoun.

Leticia decided she would try out for the team.

SUBJECTIVE

Identify the proper case for the pronoun.

If Monica joins us, the team will have enough players.

SUBJECTIVE

Identify the proper case for the pronoun.

His favorite ice cream flavor is pistachio.

POSSESSIVE

Identify the proper case for the pronoun.

Please go tell him it's time to eat.

POSSESSIVE

Identify the proper case for the pronoun.

Some families are boring, but not ours.

OBJECTIVE

Identify the proper case for the pronoun.

Their rules are pretty simple.

pronoun!

pronoun!

pronoun!

pronoun!

pronoun!

pronoun!

POSSESSIVE

Identify the proper case for the pronoun.

Is your sweater handmade?

SUBJECTIVE

Identify the proper case for the pronoun.

The decision isn't up to me.

SUBJECTIVE

Identify the proper case for the pronoun.

Did the family take her to the carnival?

DRAW TWO!

Identify the proper case for the pronoun.

Let's move them to the front of the room.

SKIP!

Identify the proper case for the pronoun.

We can't let this happen!

REVERSE!

Identify the proper case for the pronoun.

Hugo replaced the fridge after its door fell off.

PRONOUN!

PRONOUN!

PRONOUN!

PRONOUN!

PRONOUN!

PRONOUN!

OBJECTIVE

Identify the proper case for the pronoun.

It looks like a beautiful home.

OBJECTIVE

Identify the proper case for the pronoun.

This kitten must be theirs.

SUBJECTIVE

Identify the proper case for the pronoun.

The chances aren't looking good for him.

POSSESSIVE

Identify the proper case for the pronoun.

I hope this new game is fun!

SUBJECTIVE

Identify the proper case for the pronoun.

Are they here yet?

OBJECTIVE

Identify the proper case for the pronoun.

Which tuba is yours?

pronoun!

pronoun!

pronoun!

pronoun!

pronoun!

pronoun!

OBJECTIVE

Identify the proper case for the pronoun.

We love going swimming in the summer.

OBJECTIVE

Identify the proper case for the pronoun.

If we all pitch in, the project will be easy.

SUBJECTIVE

Identify the proper case for the pronoun.

Diego said he would walk Grandma home.

DRAW TWO!

Identify the proper case for the pronoun.

It is a long book, but enjoyable to read.

SKIP!

Identify the proper case for the pronoun.

This instrument is expensive, so don't drop it.

REVERSE!

Identify the proper case for the pronoun.

The principal asked us to come down to the office.

PRONOUN!

PRONOUN!

PRONOUN!

PRONOUN!

PRONOUN!

PRONOUN!

POSSESSIVE

Identify the proper case for the pronoun.

Our class is the best one in the school.

SUBJECTIVE

Identify the proper case for the pronoun.

Where are his glasses?

SUBJECTIVE

Identify the proper case for the pronoun.

The summer class will help my skills improve.

POSSESSIVE

Identify the proper case for the pronoun.

Mom isn't driving you to school this week.

POSSESSIVE

Identify the proper case for the pronoun.

She fixed the motorcycle quickly.

OBJECTIVE

Identify the proper case for the pronoun.

Mateo carried it over here.

pronoun!

pronoun!

pronoun!

pronoun!

pronoun!

pronoun!

POSSESSIVE

Identify the proper case for the pronoun.

He baked a dozen cakes.

SUBJECTIVE

Identify the proper case for the pronoun.

Let's have the party at their house.

SUBJECTIVE

Identify the proper case for the pronoun.

Let's ask her about the project.

DRAW TWO!

Identify the proper case for the pronoun.

Don't bug us while we're working.

SKIP!

Identify the proper case for the pronoun.

They just took a trip to Puerto Rico.

REVERSE!

Identify the proper case for the pronoun.

Bree made a scarf for you.

pronoun!

pronoun!

pronoun!

pronoun!

pronoun!

pronoun!

OBJECTIVE

Identify the proper case for the pronoun.

Who is moving to the neighborhood?

OBJECTIVE

Identify the proper case for the pronoun.

With whom would you like to speak?

SUBJECTIVE

Identify the proper case for the pronoun.

The choice is yours.

POSSESSIVE

Identify the proper case for the pronoun.

Give them a chance to fix the mistake.

SUBJECTIVE

Identify the proper case for the pronoun.

His calculator is missing.

OBJECTIVE

Identify the proper case for the pronoun.

Our mayor is giving a speech today.

pronoun!

pronoun!

pronoun!

pronoun!

pronoun!

pronoun!

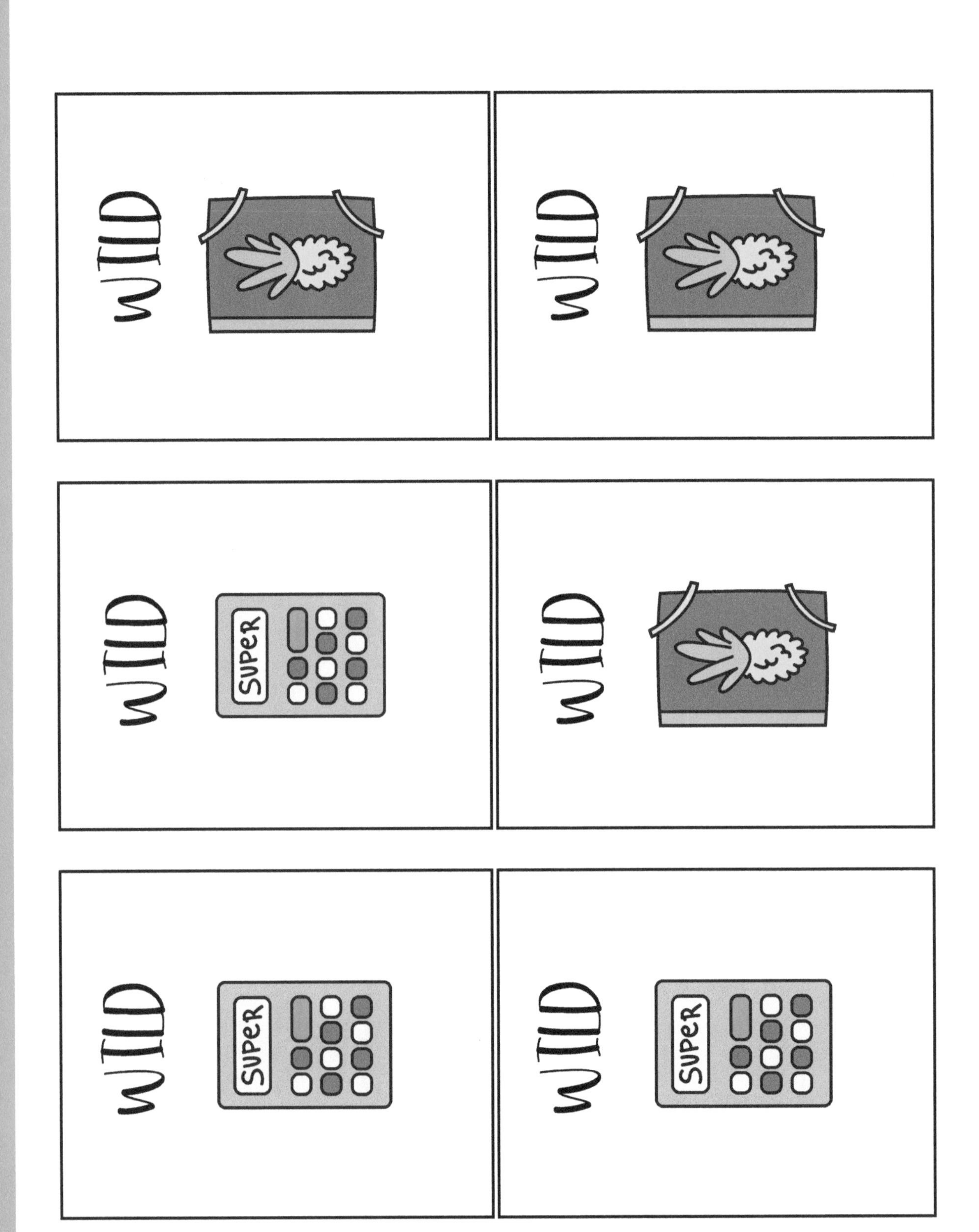
WILD
WILD
WILD
SUPER
WILD
WILD
SUPER
WILD
SUPER

pronoun!

pronoun!

pronoun!

pronoun!

pronoun!

pronoun!

WILD
draw four
WILD
draw four

WILD
draw four
WILD
draw four

WILD
draw four
WILD
draw four

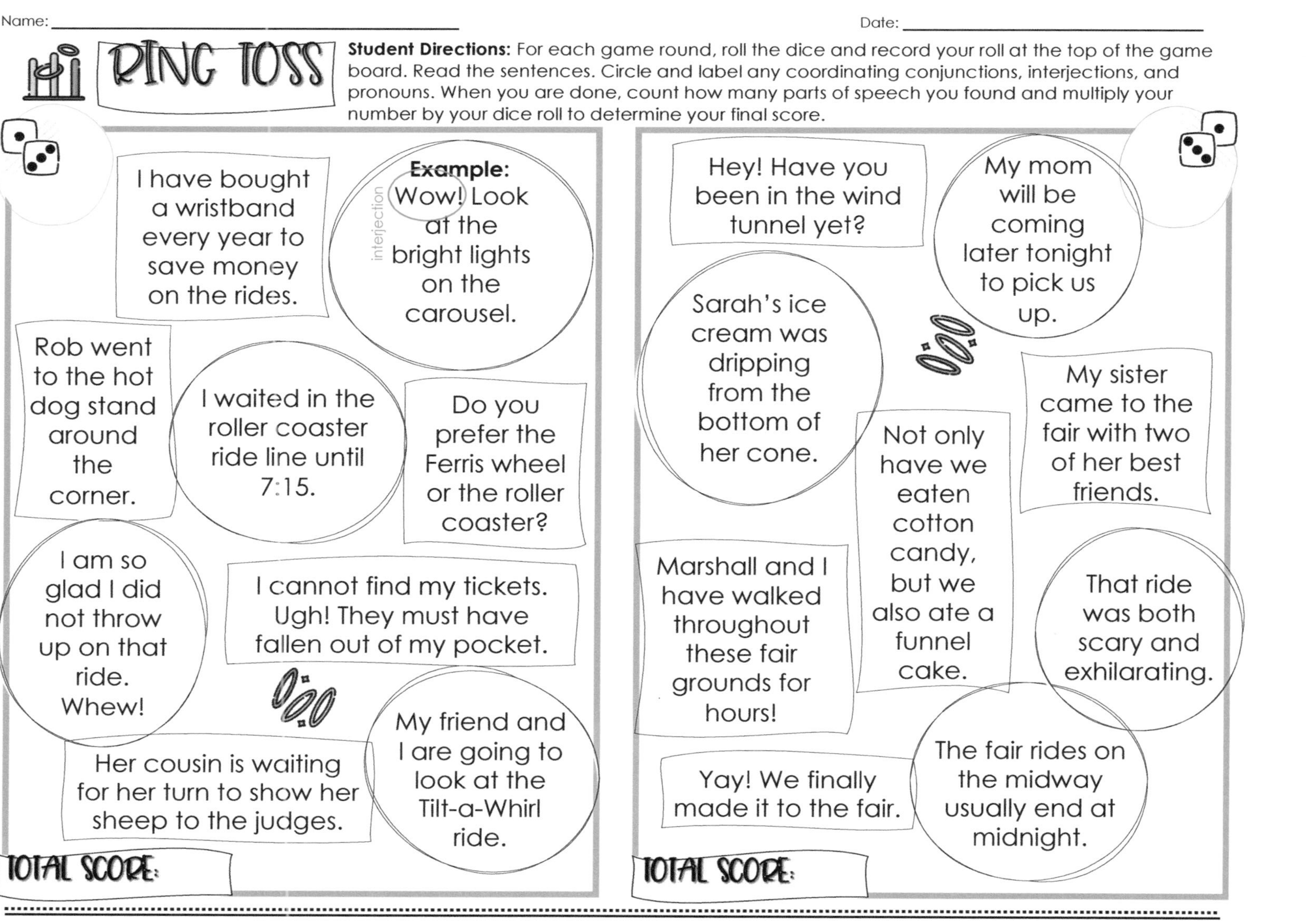

Name: ____________ Date: ____________

RING TOSS

Student Directions: For each game round, roll the dice and record your roll at the top of the game board. Read the sentences. Circle and label any coordinating conjunctions, interjections, and pronouns. When you are done, count how many parts of speech you found and multiply your number by your dice roll to determine your final score.

I have bought a wristband every year to save money on the rides.

Example: Wow! Look at the bright lights on the carousel. (interjection)

Rob went to the hot dog stand around the corner.

I waited in the roller coaster ride line until 7:15.

Do you prefer the Ferris wheel or the roller coaster?

I am so glad I did not throw up on that ride. Whew!

I cannot find my tickets. Ugh! They must have fallen out of my pocket.

Her cousin is waiting for her turn to show her sheep to the judges.

My friend and I are going to look at the Tilt-a-Whirl ride.

TOTAL SCORE:

Hey! Have you been in the wind tunnel yet?

My mom will be coming later tonight to pick us up.

Sarah's ice cream was dripping from the bottom of her cone.

My sister came to the fair with two of her best friends.

Not only have we eaten cotton candy, but we also ate a funnel cake.

Marshall and I have walked throughout these fair grounds for hours!

That ride was both scary and exhilarating.

Yay! We finally made it to the fair.

The fair rides on the midway usually end at midnight.

TOTAL SCORE:

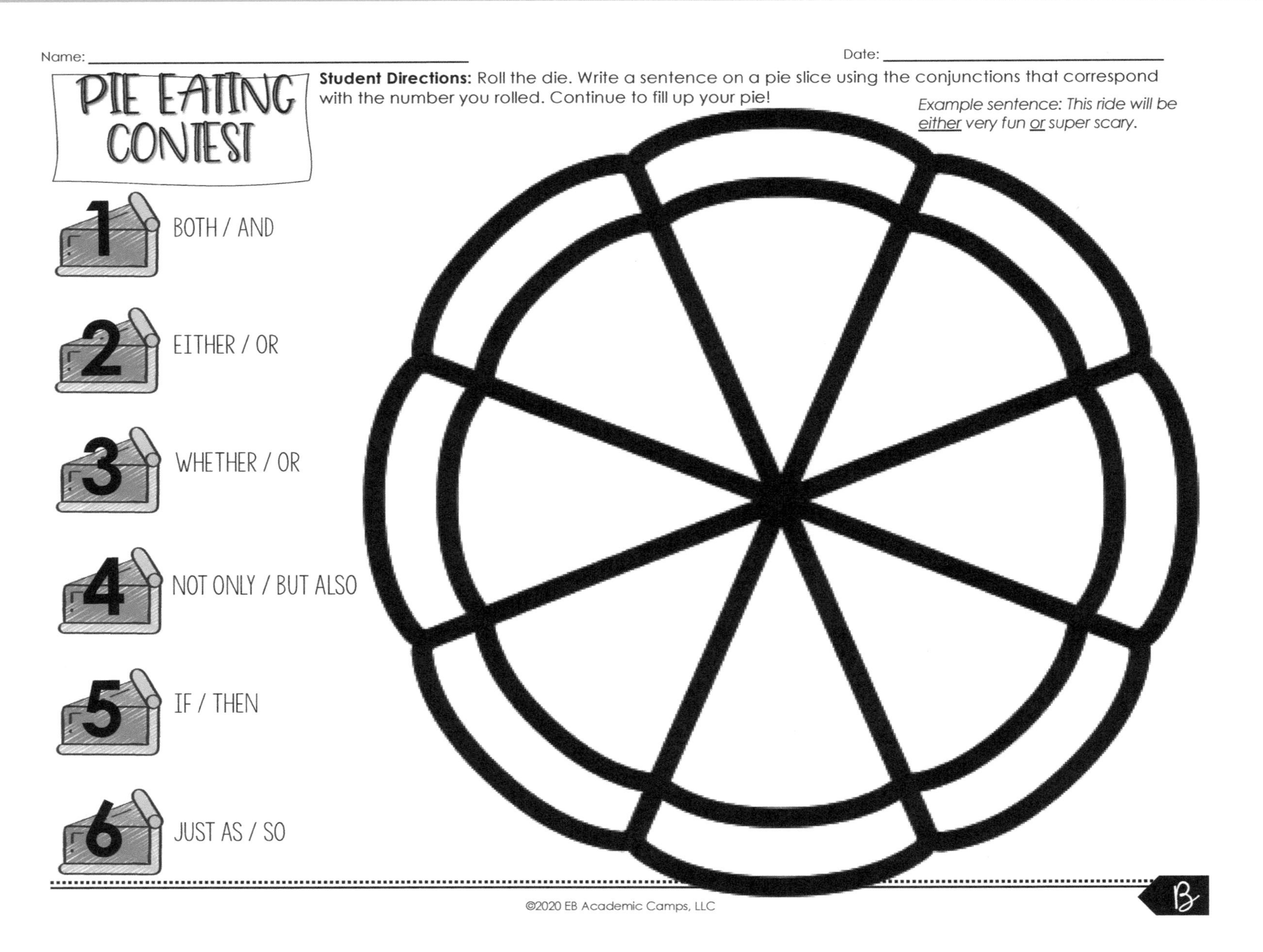

Name: ____________ Date: ____________

PIE EATING CONTEST

Student Directions: Roll the die. Write a sentence on a pie slice using the conjunctions that correspond with the number you rolled. Continue to fill up your pie!

Example sentence: This ride will be either very fun or super scary.

1 BOTH / AND

2 EITHER / OR

3 WHETHER / OR

4 NOT ONLY / BUT ALSO

5 IF / THEN

6 JUST AS / SO

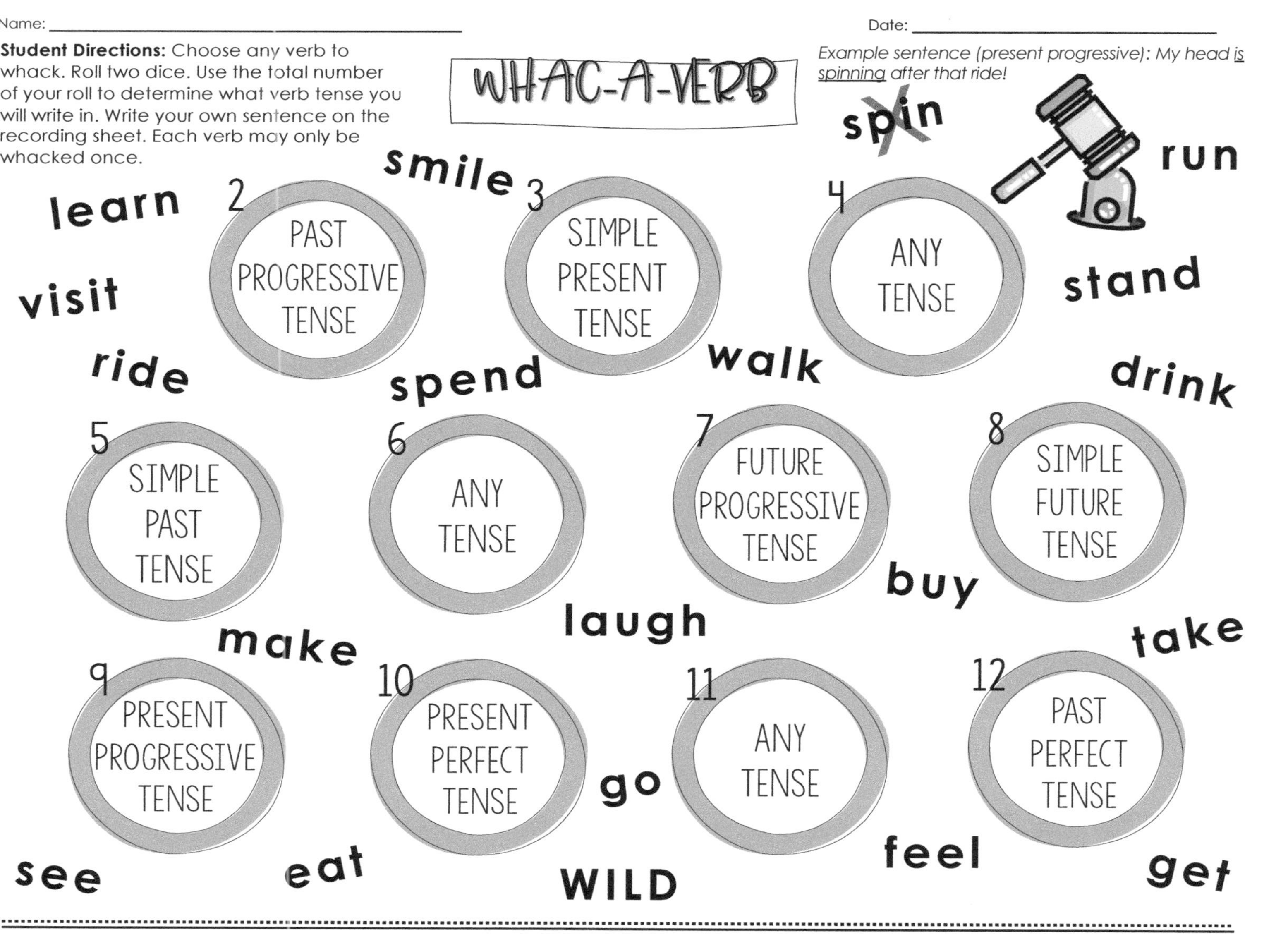
Name:
Date:
Student Directions: Choose any verb to whack. Roll two dice. Use the total number of your roll to determine what verb tense you will write in. Write your own sentence on the recording sheet. Each verb may only be whacked once.
WHAC-A-VERB
Example sentence (present progressive): My head is spinning after that ride!
spin
smile
run
learn
2 PAST PROGRESSIVE TENSE
3 SIMPLE PRESENT TENSE
4 ANY TENSE
visit
stand
ride
spend
walk
drink
5 SIMPLE PAST TENSE
6 ANY TENSE
7 FUTURE PROGRESSIVE TENSE
8 SIMPLE FUTURE TENSE
buy
laugh
make
take
9 PRESENT PROGRESSIVE TENSE
10 PRESENT PERFECT TENSE
go
11 ANY TENSE
12 PAST PERFECT TENSE
see
eat
WILD
feel
get

Name: ______________________ Date: ____________

RECORDING SHEET

Student Directions: Write your sentences here using the verb you whacked in the tense that you rolled.

1.

2.

3.

4.

5.

6.

7.

8.

Name: ______________________ Date: ____________

RECORDING SHEET

Student Directions: Write your sentences here using the verb you whacked in the tense that you rolled.

1.

2.

3.

4.

5.

6.

7.

8.

Name: ______________________ Date: ______________________

BALLOON DARTS

Student Directions: Pop an antecedent balloon by placing an "X" over it. Use that antecedent in a sentence with a pronoun. Try to connect four balloons in a row. In order to count, your four sentences must use four different pronoun types. Record your sentences on the recording sheet.

CORN DOGS	MONICA	HORSE	VENDOR	SWINGS
FRIEND	SHOE (X)	ROLLER COASTER	SNOW CONE	GAME
WRISTBAND	KETCHUP	FAIR	PRIZE	LIGHTS
FERRIS WHEEL	BRYSON	MONEY	FAMILY	FRENCH FRIES

Name: ______________________ Date: ______________________

RECORDING SHEET

Student Directions: Pop a balloon to determine what antecedent to use in your sentence. In order to connect four balloons in a row, your four sentences must use four different pronoun types. Record your sentences on this sheet for each game. Underline the antecedent in each sentence once and the pronoun(s) twice.

pronoun types

SUBJECT PRONOUN	INTENSIVE PRONOUN
OBJECT PRONOUN	POSSESSIVE PRONOUN
REFLEXIVE PRONOUN	POSSESSIVE ADJECTIVE

GAME 1

Example: I got gum on my shoe, and it is ruined. (object pronoun for shoe)

1.

2.

3.

4.

GAME 2

1.

2.

3.

4.

Name: ______________________ Date: ______________________

BUMPER CARS

Student Directions: Roll two dice. The first roll will determine your interjection and the second roll will determine your emotion. Bump the two together to create a complete sentence. Record your sentences in the space below.

interjection

1. YIKES!
2. BRAVO!
3. HEY!
4. OOPS!
5. UGH!
6. CREATE YOUR OWN

emotion

1. AGREEMENT
2. SADNESS
3. ANGER
4. CREATE YOUR OWN
5. HAPPINESS
6. SURPRISE

Example sentence: Yes! We are next in line. (happiness)

1.
2.
3.
4.
5.
6.
7.
8.
9.
10.

Escape Room

instructions for use

In this interactive abandoned house escape room, students will do a close reading of a short story and analyze figurative language, plot, and characterization. They will work through a maze, answer close reading questions, complete a plot elements scavenger hunt, answer character analysis questions, and solve an encrypted code! The instructions below outline each step of this escape room lesson.

Before the Lesson:

1. To set up your classroom for this activity, you might consider doing a mini room transformation by hanging jaggedly cut plastic tablecloths over the windows, pinning some fake cobwebs to the corners of the room, and playing haunted house sounds on YouTube! This is all completely optional and students will be engaged in the lesson regardless!
2. Prior to running the escape room, you will need to print out a copy of the **Escape Room Student Booklet** for each member of the class. You will also want one copy of the **Escape Room Answer Key** for yourself so you can quickly check student answers and help struggling groups.
3. You will also need to print out the **Plot Cards**. There must be enough plot cards for the number of student groups completing the escape room.
4. Separate each plot point card into similar piles (All of the #1 cards in one pile, #2 cards in another pile, etc.) and place each set of plot point cards in different envelopes. Label each envelope "Plot Card." These will be hidden around your classroom, and students will be searching for them to solve one of the puzzles.
5. It is up to you where you hide them in the classroom. We like to make it a bit challenging, and put them in unexpected places.
6. *Note: There are a total of 12 plot point cards each group will be collecting, but only 7 of them actually correlate to the plot structure of the story. It is the numbers on those particular cards that will reveal the code students need.*

Escape Room

instructions for use

During the Lesson:

1. Tell students that they will be participating in an escape room. Divide them into small groups (we recommend 3-4 students maximum) and explain that they will need to work with their teammates to solve puzzles that relate to a common text. Although the first three groups to escape the abandoned house the quickest will win prizes, all groups must complete every task. In addition, every student must actively contribute to solving each puzzle.

2. Pass out an **Escape Room Student Booklet** to each class member. We recommend reading the Your Mission section aloud to students and answering any clarifying questions before they begin the escape room.

3. As students begin to work through each of the escape room challenges, informally assess students for participation and effort. Keep your **Escape Room Answer Key** ready to provide hints for groups that get stuck. You will also need to approve answers from each student group as they complete each task in the escape room.

4. Have fun! Though escape rooms can take some time to set up on the front end, they are a magical experience for students! Play up the abandoned house theme and enjoy watching students be incredibly engaged!

5. For the first three winners of the escape room, you may choose to give a prize, such as a fun pack of pencils, a piece of candy, or a homework pass. You decide!

THE MOVING UP
challenge
ESCAPE ROOM BOOKLET
STUDENT NAME: ______

ENCRYPTED CODE

Nice work! Solve this next puzzle, and you'll get the key to escape this house once and for all! Who knows? Maybe you'll be the headline in a future article of the *Franklinville Junior High Gazette*! "Student Successfully Escapes Abandoned Home in Record Time" has a nice ring to it, don't you think?

Directions: Look through every answer page in your "Moving Up Challenge" booklet. On these pages, you will find eight unique symbols. Circle those symbols below. Then, use the key and the hints to your code phrase to discover the message that will finally allow you to escape this abandoned house!

SYMBOLS KEY

Use the key below to discover the message that will allow you to escape this abandoned house! ***Hint: it might be more than one word!***

┤	⇔	⏢	⏀	+	⌒	⌗	⌊	Ö	┐	□
R	V	A	I	S	P	E	O	!	F	T

Code Phrase:

⌒ ⌊ ⇔ ⏀ Ö

___ ___ ___ ___ ___ ___ ___ ___

11

CHARACTERS

Write the answer to each question from page 9 in the boxes below.

***If your answer has more than one word, enter both in the answer boxes WITHOUT a space. You won't always need every box.

1.

2.

3.

4.

5.

6.

7.

Unscramble the letters to describe how the bullies *wanted* May to feel.

Record answer letters here: *(Unscramble to reveal the code word and enter it in the boxes below)*

CODE WORD:

YOUR MISSION

It all started last week when you were in the library studying for finals. You took a quick break and looked through some of the old editions of the *Franklinville Junior High Gazette* that the librarian had lying out on the display counter. One article in particular, caught your eye...

(Turn to pages 5 and 6 and read "The Moving Up Challenge" article. Then come right back here!)

You put down the newspaper and nervously started collecting your thoughts. You're new to Franklinville Junior High, and unfortunately, this May girl who supposedly put an end to the Moving Up Challenge, graduated years ago. Over the years, students have brought back this tradition, and they've been hyping up this year's challenge for the last few weeks. You're dreading your turn in the abandoned house on Merridy Lane, but it seems better than being treated like a lower grade student all of next year!

So, you've accepted the challenge and are spending the night in the abandoned house all by yourself. The students at Franklinville Junior High have gotten pretty clever over the years, and now require any student who takes on the Moving Up Challenge to solve a series of puzzles if they want to escape the abandoned house on Merridy Lane.

Of course, you're up for the challenge! This booklet contains all the puzzles you must solve.

Each time you successfully complete a puzzle, **submit your finished work to your teacher** to receive your next set of instructions.

The first three groups to escape win a prize! (However, all groups must complete all the puzzles and every member of the group must actively participate in each task!)

Check out the next page for your first puzzle! Good luck, and make sure not to share answers with other groups!

YOUR FIRST TASK

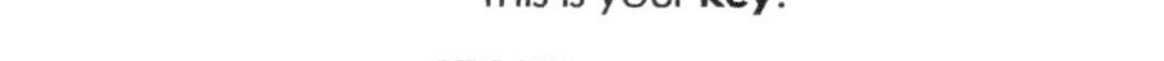

Solve this maze. Once you do, collect the letters you find along your path. These spell out a code word. This is your **key**.

START

FINISH

KEY WORD: ________________________

4

Your exploration of the abandoned house went well! It appears you're going to impress everyone at Franklinville Junior High with your puzzle solving skills. In fact, you may just be able to escape this place pretty soon! But first, it's time to do a little detective work. Answer seven character questions and use your answers to unlock your next code!

CHARACTERS

1. Identify the character who says the following: "It's just some dumb dare that kids came up with years ago. I had forgotten all about it, and I'm sure most people have, too. They only challenge the new kids at school, and you don't even seem like a new kid anymore."
   a. Steffie
   b. May
   c. A bully
2. May is the ___________ of the story
   a. Protagonist
   b. Antagonist
   c. Minor Character
3. The following quote demonstrates that Steffie is:
   "Of course I wouldn't treat you like a seventh-grader," Steffie assured May, as they were ready to become eighth-graders.
   a. Friendly
   b. Loyal
   c. Competitive
4. The following quotation from the story demonstrates that May is:
   "When school resumed in the fall, May made a point of seeking out and befriending any new kids. She kept her ears open for any talk about the moving up challenge."
   a. Caring
   b. Generous
   c. Curious
5. Steffie is a ___________ character in the story.
   a. Main
   b. Evil
   c. Supporting
6. May's determination to stand up to the bullies in her class shows:
   a. Determination
   b. Doubt
   c. Confidence
7. May is targeted for the moving up challenge because she is:
   a. A girl
   b. Mean
   c. New

9

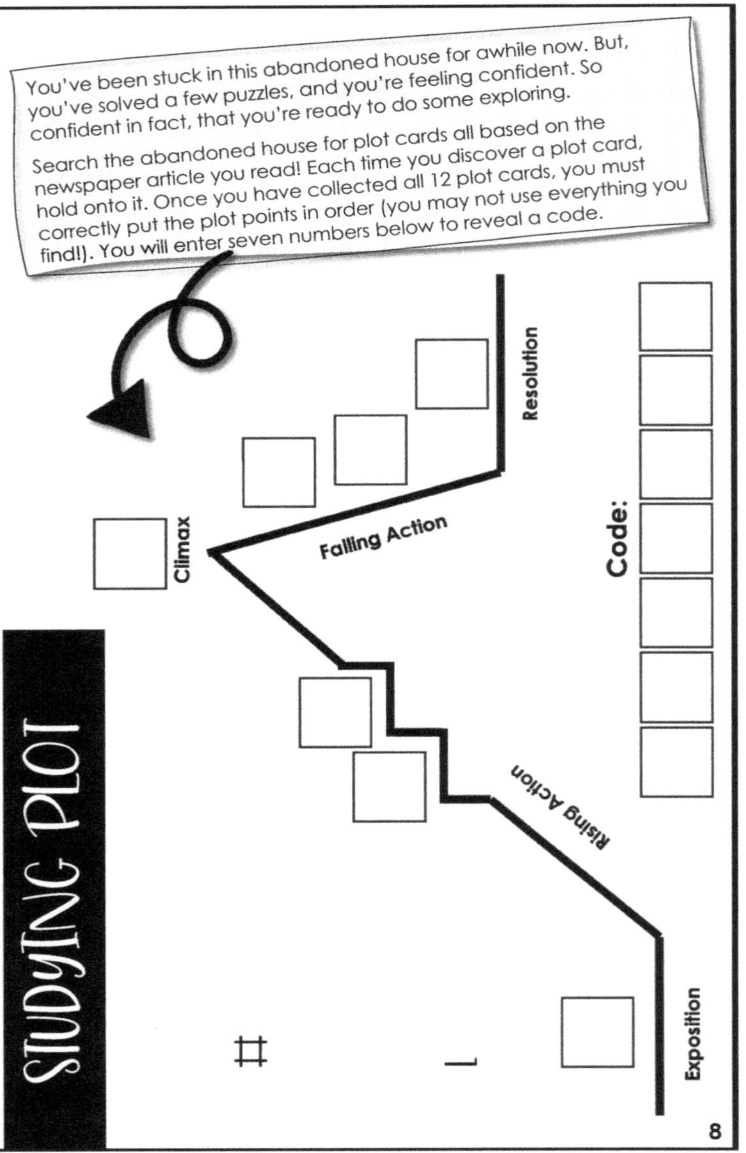

CLOSE READING

Now it's time to reread the newspaper article you found. In order to solve this next puzzle, you must answer all the questions on the following page correctly and use the letters associated with the answers to unscramble a word.

Everyone in Franklinville seemed to be enjoying the long-awaited spring weather after winter had clung to the calendar like the icicles clung to roofs well into April. Days were finally long and sunny, flowers had broken through the soil, and neighbors were out enjoying the end of their hibernation. Yes, everyone was happy May had come, except for May herself.

This should have been the most exciting time of May's school year. After transferring into Franklinville Junior High in October, she had worked her fingers to the bone to keep her grades up and to make friends. It should have been time for May to celebrate making high honor roll, being chosen for first chair for violin in the orchestra, and winning vice president in the student council election. Instead of enjoying her accomplishments and studying for final exams, though, May could only think about one thing – the moving up challenge.

Steffie, May's best friend, explained the challenge to her one day as they walked home from school together.

"It's just some dumb dare that kids came up with years ago. I had forgotten all about it, and I'm sure most people have, too. They only challenge the new kids at school, and you don't even seem like a new kid anymore."

Thoughts of the moving up challenge bounced around May's head like a pinball – sneaking into the abandoned house, taking a picture in every room, not coming out until morning. It seemed ridiculous that anyone would agree to take such a dare, until you considered the consequences of chickening out. Anyone new to Franklinville Junior High who didn't complete the challenge before Moving Up Day wouldn't move up with their class. Sure, their classes and teachers would all go on as expected, but that person would be treated as part of the grade below by all his or her classmates.

"Of course I wouldn't treat you like a seventh-grader," Steffie assured May, as they were ready to become eighth-graders. "And besides, you'll be our student council vice president – kind of hard to ignore that."

May wasn't so sure the zombies in her seventh-grade class would think as independently as Steffie. The truth was, May wasn't really afraid of going into the abandoned house alone for a night. It was more the principle of the challenge that bothered her. Anyone who would bully a new kid into doing something scary and possibly dangerous deserved a taste of their own medicine. May had just the plan.

5

As she had announced to several classmates, May prepared to spend the night in the abandoned house on Saturday, June 3. She had a sleeping bag and her smartphone camera ready, and her parents thought she was sleeping at Steffie's house.

When May arrived at the abandoned house on that Saturday night, she could see members of the bully squad setting up tents around the house at a distance. Some were just there for the excitement of the event, but others were there to make sure May went through with the challenge. She entered the home through a broken basement window. It probably would've been frightening if she wasn't so excited about carrying out her plan.

For several hours, May talked on the phone with Steffie and played games on her phone. She didn't make any effort to explore the house or take pictures. Late into the night, when she was sure the bullies would be asleep, May crept out into the darkness. She approached the first tent wearing a rubber mask she'd packed just for this occasion. With her camera ready, she gave a roar and snapped pictures of her classmates' frightened faces. Then she hurried back to the shelter of the abandoned house.

When the excitement died down, and the night was quiet again, May repeated her stunt. One after another, she scared the small groups of classmates who had camped out. By sunrise, May's phone was filled with pictures of terrorized faces.

Moving Up Day went ahead as scheduled, and May received many honors. All summer long, May heard murmurings about the photos she'd taken. "You erased those, right?" "What is she planning to do with them?" But May's lips were sealed.

When school resumed in the fall, May made a point of seeking out and befriending any new kids. She kept her ears open for any talk about the moving up challenge. Whenever the topic came up, she reassured the new kid with hilarious pictures of the bullies, and she reminded the bullies that if they went through with the challenge, she'd make their pictures famous. After that fall, the moving up challenge disappeared from Franklinville Junior High for good.

By April LoTempio

Record answer letters here: (Unscramble to reveal the code word and enter it in the boxes below)

CODE WORD: | | | | | | | | |

6

1. Which image from the opening paragraph is used as a simile?
   a. enjoying the long-awaited spring weather
   b. winter had clung to the calendar
   c. days were finally long and sunny
   d. flowers had broken through the soil

2. In the text, May thinks of her seventh-grade classmates as "zombies." What type of figurative language is this?
   v. personification
   w. hyperbole
   x. simile
   y. metaphor

3. Which example of figurative language from the text is a different type than the other three?
   f. worked her fingers to the bone
   g. bounced around May's head like a pinball
   h. a taste of their own medicine
   i. May's lips were sealed

4. The text says, "until you considered the consequences of chickening out." The use of the phrase "chickening out" implies what about the challenge?
   j. A person who does the challenge will feel like a chicken in a coop.
   k. Most people would do the challenge with a friend but not alone.
   l. The only reason someone wouldn't do it is because he or she is afraid.
   m. Turning down the challenge would be worse than the consequences of doing it.

5. The text says, "Anyone who would bully a new kid into doing something." Suppose the words "bully/into" were replaced with "persuade/to." How would this change the connotation?
   n. It would make the "Anyone" seem not so mean.
   o. It would make the "Anyone" seem more abusive.
   p. It would make the new kid seem more like a wimp.
   q. It would make the new kid seem harder to convince.

6. The text says that someone wouldn't consider doing the challenge until they considered the consequences. What detail from the text supports this claim?
   i. Students camped out around the house to see if May would stay inside.
   j. May was able to put a stop to the challenge from then on.
   k. No one has ever chickened out of doing the challenge before.
   l. The consequence is being treated like a member of the class one grade below.

7. Which detail from the text supports the inference that Steffie is a good friend to May?
   s. Steffie goes with May into the house to keep her company.
   t. Steffie tries to talk the bullies out of making May do the challenge.
   u. Steffie promises not to treat May differently if she doesn't do the challenge.
   v. Steffie scares the bullies who are camped out around the house.

8. Which detail from the text supports the inference that May is clever?
   h. She is elected vice president of the student council.
   i. She uses the moving up challenge to scare the bullies.
   j. She seeks out new kids at school to become their friend.
   k. She makes the bullies think she stayed in the house all night.

7

THE MOVING UP
challenge
ESCAPE ROOM BOOKLET
STUDENT NAME: ____________

ENCRYPTED CODE

Nice work! Solve this next puzzle, and you'll get the key to escape this house once and for all! Who knows? Maybe you'll be the headline in a future article of the *Franklinville Junior High Gazette*! "Student Successfully Escapes Abandoned Home in Record Time" has a nice ring to it, don't you think?

Directions: Look through every answer page in your "Moving Up Challenge" booklet. On these pages, you will find eight unique symbols. Circle those symbols below. Then, use the key and the hints to your code phrase to discover the message that will finally allow you to escape this abandoned house!

SYMBOLS KEY

Use the key below to discover the message that will allow you to escape this abandoned house! *Hint: it might be more than one word!*

R V A I S P E O ! F T

Code Phrase:

P R O V E I T !

CHARACTERS

Write the answer to each question from page 9 in the boxes below.

***If your answer has more than one word, enter both in the answer boxes WITHOUT a space. You won't always need every box.

1. S T E F F I E
2. P R O T A G O N I S T
3. L O Y A L
4. C A R I N G
5. S U P P O R T I N G
6. C O N F I D E N C E
7. N E W

Unscramble the letters to describe how the bullies *wanted* May to feel.

Record answer letters here: *(Unscramble to reveal the code word and enter it in the boxes below)*

CODE WORD:

F E A R F U L

YOUR MISSION

It all started last week when you were in the library studying for finals. You took a quick break and looked through some of the old editions of the *Franklinville Junior High Gazette* that the librarian had lying out on the display counter. One article in particular, caught your eye...

(Turn to pages 5 and 6 and read "The Moving Up Challenge" article. Then come right back here!)

You put down the newspaper and nervously started collecting your thoughts. You're new to Franklinville Junior High, and unfortunately, this May girl who supposedly put an end to the Moving Up Challenge, graduated years ago. Over the years, students have brought back this tradition, and they've been hyping up this year's challenge for the last few weeks. You're dreading your turn in the abandoned house on Merridy Lane, but it seems better than being treated like a lower grade student all of next year!

So, you've accepted the challenge and are spending the night in the abandoned house all by yourself. The students at Franklinville Junior High have gotten pretty clever over the years, and now require any student who takes on the Moving Up Challenge to solve a series of puzzles if they want to escape the abandoned house on Merridy Lane.

Of course, you're up for the challenge! This booklet contains all the puzzles you must solve.

Each time you successfully complete a puzzle, **submit your finished work to your teacher** to receive your next set of instructions.

The first three groups to escape win a prize! (However, all groups must complete all the puzzles and every member of the group must actively participate in each task!)

Check out the next page for your first puzzle! Good luck, and make sure not to share answers with other groups!

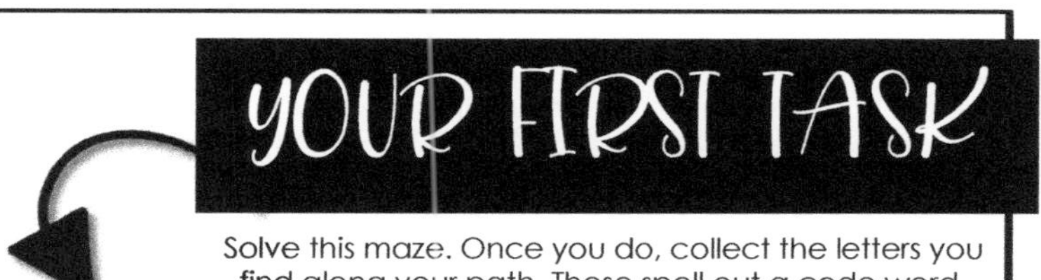
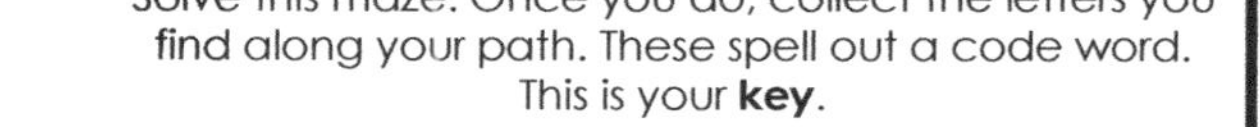
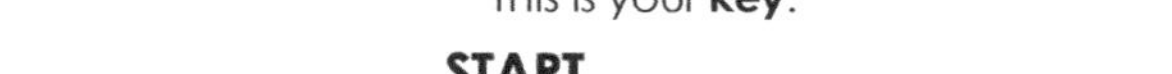

YOUR FIRST TASK

Solve this maze. Once you do, collect the letters you find along your path. These spell out a code word. This is your **key**.

START

FINISH

KEY WORD: CHALLENGE

4

Your exploration of the abandoned house went well! It appears you're going to impress everyone at Franklinville Junior High with your puzzle solving skills. In fact, you may just be able to escape this place pretty soon! But first, it's time to do a little detective work. Answer seven character questions and use your answers to unlock your next code!

CHARACTERS

1. Identify the character who says the following: "It's just some dumb **dare** that kids came up with years ago. I had forgotten all about it, and I'm sure most people have, too. They only challenge the new kids at school, and you don't even seem like a new kid anymore."
   a. **Steffie**
   b. May
   c. A bully
2. May is the ___________ of the story
   a. **Protagonist**
   b. Antagonist
   c. Minor Character
3. The following quote demonstrates that Steffie is:
   "Of course I wouldn't treat you like a seventh-grader," Steffie assured May, as they were ready to become eighth-graders.
   a. Friendly
   b. **Loyal**
   c. Competitive
4. The following quotation from the story demonstrates that May is:
   "When school resumed in the fall, May made a point of seeking out and befriending any new kids. She kept her ears open for any talk about the moving up challenge."
   a. **Caring**
   b. Generous
   c. Curious
5. Steffie is a ____________ character in the story.
   a. Main
   b. Evil
   c. **Supporting**
6. May's determination to stand up to the bullies in her class shows:
   a. Determination
   b. Doubt
   c. **Confidence**
7. May is targeted for the moving up challenge because she is:
   a. A girl
   b. Mean
   c. **New**

9

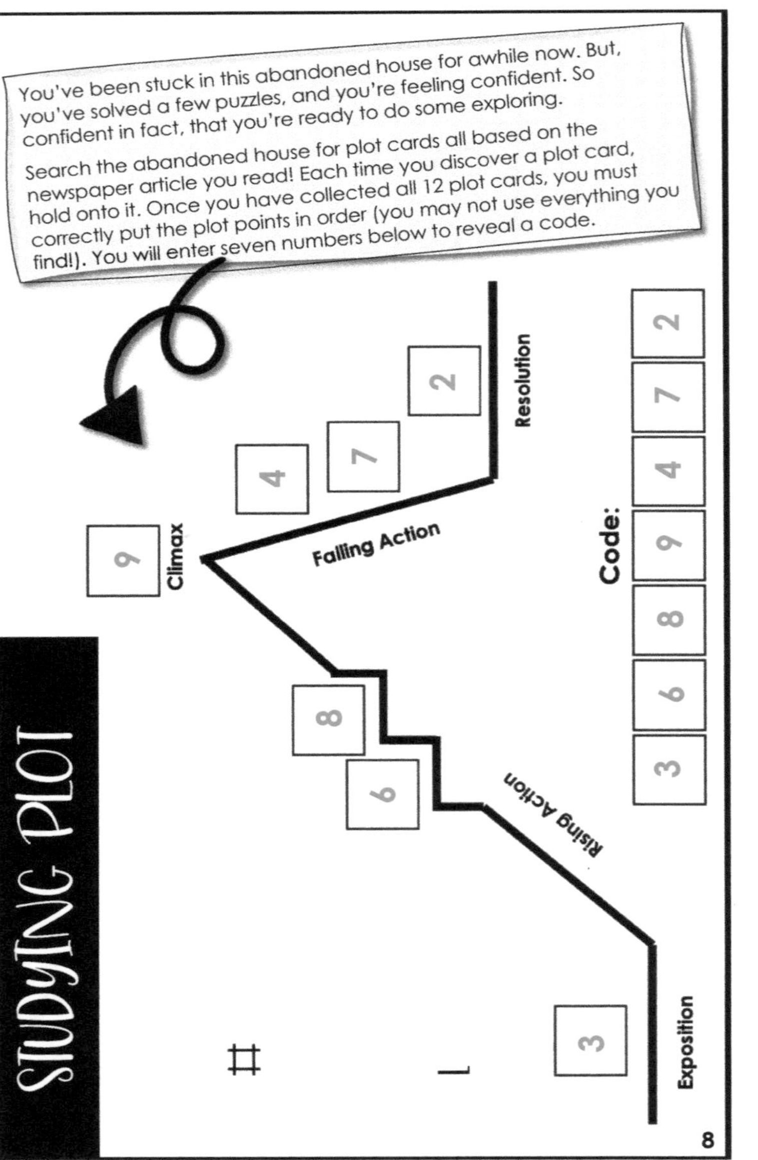

CLOSE READING

Now it's time to reread the newspaper article you found. In order to solve this next puzzle, you must answer all these questions on the following page correctly and use the letters associated with the answers to unscramble a word.

Everyone in Franklinville seemed to be enjoying the long-awaited spring weather after winter had clung to the calendar like the icicles clung to roofs well into April. Days were finally long and sunny, flowers had broken through the soil, and neighbors were out enjoying the end of their hibernation. Yes, everyone was happy May had come, except for May herself.

This should have been the most exciting time of May's school year. After transferring into Franklinville Junior High in October, she had worked her fingers to the bone to keep her grades up and to make friends. It should have been time for May to celebrate making high honor roll, being chosen for first chair for violin in the orchestra, and winning vice president in the student council election. Instead of enjoying her accomplishments and studying for final exams, though, May could only think about one thing – the moving up challenge.

Steffie, May's best friend, explained the challenge to her one day as they walked home from school together.

"It's just some dumb dare that kids came up with years ago. I had forgotten all about it, and I'm sure most people have, too. They only challenge the new kids at school, and you don't even seem like a new kid anymore."

Thoughts of the moving up challenge bounced around May's head like a pinball – sneaking into the abandoned house, taking a picture in every room, not coming out until morning. It seemed ridiculous that anyone would agree to take such a dare, until you considered the consequences of chickening out. Anyone new to Franklinville Junior High who didn't complete the challenge before Moving Up Day wouldn't move up with their class. Sure, their classes and teachers would all go on as expected, but that person would be treated as part of the grade below by all his or her classmates.

"Of course I wouldn't treat you like a seventh-grader," Steffie assured May, as they were ready to become eighth-graders. "And besides, you'll be our student council vice president – kind of hard to ignore that."

May wasn't so sure the zombies in her seventh-grade class would think as independently as Steffie. The truth was, May wasn't really afraid of going into the abandoned house alone for a night. It was more the principle of the challenge that bothered her. Anyone who would bully a new kid into doing something scary and possibly dangerous deserved a taste of their own medicine. May had just the plan.

5

As she had announced to several classmates, May prepared to spend the night in the abandoned house on Saturday, June 3. She had a sleeping bag and her smartphone camera ready, and her parents thought she was sleeping at Steffie's house.

When May arrived at the abandoned house on that Saturday night, she could see members of the bully squad setting up tents around the house at a distance. Some were just there for the excitement of the event, but others were there to make sure May went through with the challenge. She entered the home through a broken basement window. It probably would've been frightening if she wasn't so excited about carrying out her plan.

For several hours, May talked on the phone with Steffie and played games on her phone. She didn't make any effort to explore the house or take pictures. Late into the night, when she was sure the bullies would be asleep, May crept out into the darkness. She approached the first tent wearing a rubber mask she'd packed just for this occasion. With her camera ready, she gave a roar and snapped pictures of her classmates' frightened faces. Then she hurried back to the shelter of the abandoned house.

When the excitement died down, and the night was quiet again, May repeated her stunt. One after another, she scared the small groups of classmates who had camped out. By sunrise, May's phone was filled with pictures of terrorized faces.

Moving Up Day went ahead as scheduled, and May received many honors. All summer long, May heard murmurings about the photos she'd taken. "You erased those, right?" "What is she planning to do with them?" But May's lips were sealed.

When school resumed in the fall, May made a point of seeking out and befriending any new kids. She kept her ears open for any talk about the moving up challenge. Whenever the topic came up, she reassured the new kid with hilarious pictures of the bullies, and she reminded the bullies that if they went through with the challenge, she'd make their pictures famous. After that fall, the moving up challenge disappeared from Franklinville Junior High for good.

By April LoTempio

Record answer letters here: (Unscramble to reveal the code word and enter it in the boxes below)

CODE WORD: B U L L Y I N G

6

1. Which image from the opening paragraph is used as a simile?
   a. enjoying the long-awaited spring weather
   b. winter had clung to the calendar
   c. Days were finally long and sunny
   d. flowers had broken through the soil

2. In the text, May thinks of her seventh-grade classmates as "zombies." What type of figurative language is this?
   v. personification
   w. hyperbole
   x. simile
   y. metaphor

3. Which example of figurative language from the text is a different type than the other three?
   f. worked her fingers to the bone (idiom)
   g. bounced around May's head like a pinball (simile)
   h. a taste of their own medicine (idiom)
   i. May's lips were sealed (idiom)

4. The text says, "until you considered the consequences of chickening out." The use of the phrase "chickening out" implies what about the challenge?
   j. A person who does the challenge will feel like a chicken in a coop.
   k. Most people would do the challenge with a friend but not alone.
   l. The only reason someone wouldn't do it is because he or she is afraid.
   m. Turning down the challenge would be worse than the consequences of doing it.

5. The text says, "Anyone who would bully a new kid into doing something." Suppose the words "bully/into" were replaced with "persuade/to." How would this change the connotation?
   n. It would make the "Anyone" seem not so mean.
   o. It would make the "Anyone" seem more abusive.
   p. It would make the new kid seem more like a wimp.
   q. It would make the new kid seem harder to convince.

6. The text says that someone wouldn't consider doing the challenge until they considered the consequences. What detail from the text supports this claim?
   i. Students camped out around the house to see if May would stay inside.
   j. May was able to put a stop to the challenge from then on.
   k. No one has ever chickened out of doing the challenge before.
   l. The consequence is being treated like a member of the class one grade below.

7. Which detail from the text supports the inference that Steffie is a good friend to May?
   s. Steffie goes with May into the house to keep her company.
   t. Steffie tries to talk the bullies out of making May do the challenge.
   u. Steffie promises not to treat May differently if she doesn't do the challenge.
   v. Steffie scares the bullies who are camped out around the house.

8. Which detail from the text supports the inference that May is clever?
   h. She is elected vice president of the student council.
   i. She uses the moving up challenge to scare the bullies.
   j. She seeks out new kids at school to become their friend.
   k. She makes the bullies think she stayed in the house all night.

7

1. PLOT CARD

May and her best friend entered the abandoned house together.

2. PLOT CARD

The moving up challenge stopped occurring.

3. PLOT CARD

Spring had sprung in Franklinville.

4. PLOT CARD

The bullies hoped that May deleted all the photos she took of them.

5. PLOT CARD

May is a strong-willed character.

6. PLOT CARD

Steffie explained the moving up challenge to May.

7. PLOT CARD

May befriended and reassured all new Franklinville students.

8. PLOT CARD

May told her parents she was sleeping over at Steffie's and went to the abandoned house.

9. PLOT CARD

May scared the bullies camping outside the house and photographed them.

10. PLOT CARD

The bullies threatened to steal May's camera.

11. PLOT CARD

The winter metaphor emphasizes the late spring arrival.

12. PLOT CARD

A theme of the story is that you should treat others how you want to be treated.

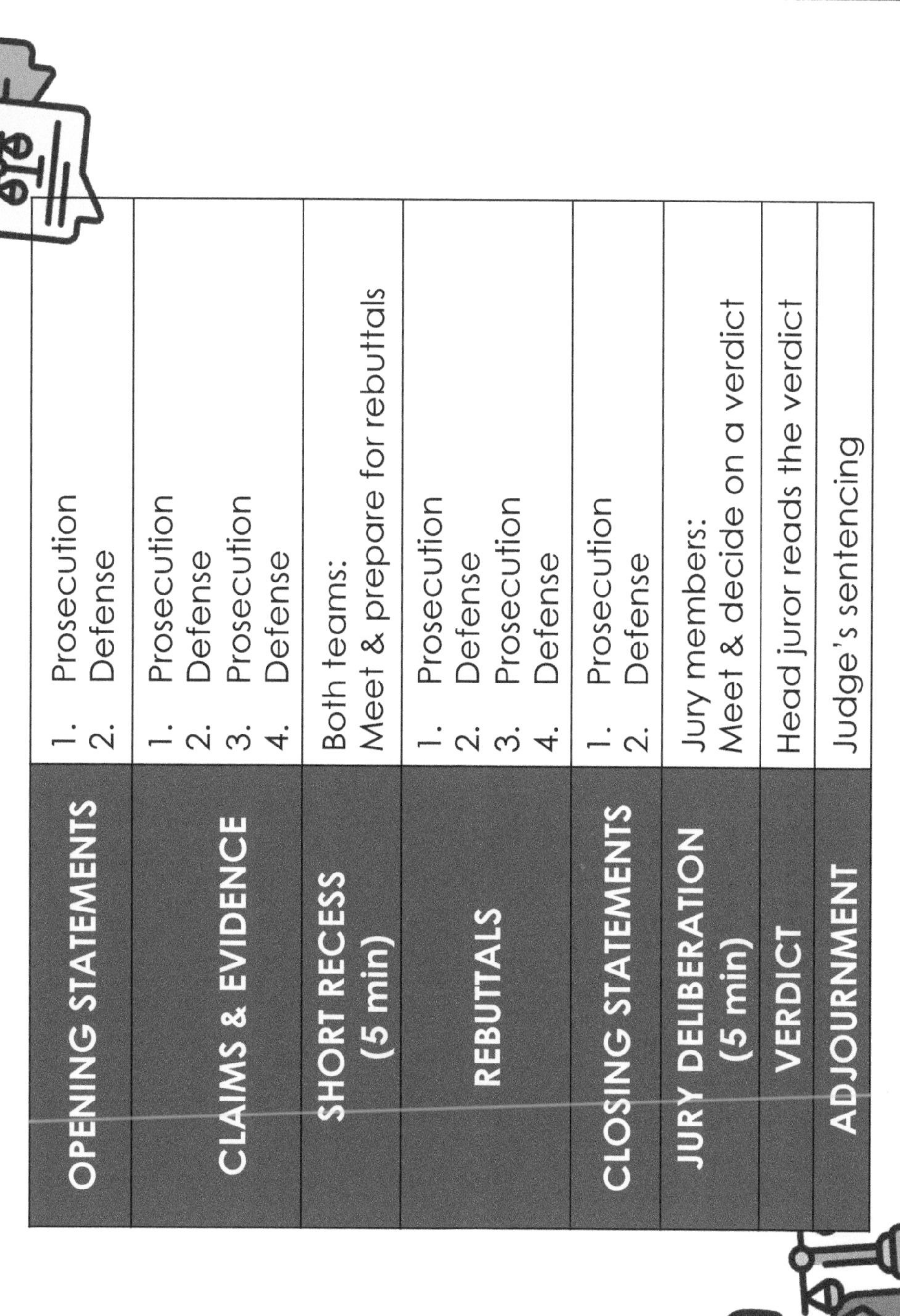

Mock Trial Agenda

OPENING STATEMENTS	1. Prosecution 2. Defense
CLAIMS & EVIDENCE	1. Prosecution 2. Defense 3. Prosecution 4. Defense
SHORT RECESS (5 min)	Both teams: Meet & prepare for rebuttals
REBUTTALS	1. Prosecution 2. Defense 3. Prosecution 4. Defense
CLOSING STATEMENTS	1. Prosecution 2. Defense
JURY DELIBERATION (5 min)	Jury members: Meet & decide on a verdict
VERDICT	Head juror reads the verdict
ADJOURNMENT	Judge's sentencing

Name ______________________ Date ______________________

Opening Statement

Student Directions: Your task is to give an overview of the case to the jury. You can use quotes from the story and allude to some of the evidence your team will be sharing, but you do not want to give everything away! You should only be presenting the facts! Read the tips and tricks below and jot down notes to include in your opening statement. Read the example opening statement for inspiration.

Capture!

Capture the audience's attention by immediately presenting the theme of the case.

Tell!

Tell a story that paints your client in the best possible light. Using metaphors and descriptive language can help enhance the story and engage jurors.

Connect!

Make a connection with the jury! Don't simply read your opening statement.

Conclude!

End your opening statement by telling the jury the action you would like them to take at the end of the trial. Ask them to rule in your favor!

Example of an Opening Statement

Ladies and gentlemen of the jury, my name is Clyde Haynes, and I am representing Martha Washington. Martha, an upstanding citizen, mother, wife, and former school teacher, is unfortunately being painted as a villain in this case. After taking some time off of work to care for her dying mother, Martha came back to her position to find out that her replacement had mismanaged funds and done so under Ms. Washington's name. This is simply a case of a kind woman who has put all her efforts into her work and family, only to be falsely accused by her employer, Mr. Gaines. In this trial, we ask you to really examine the evidence. You will clearly see that my client has done nothing wrong.

Your Opening Statement

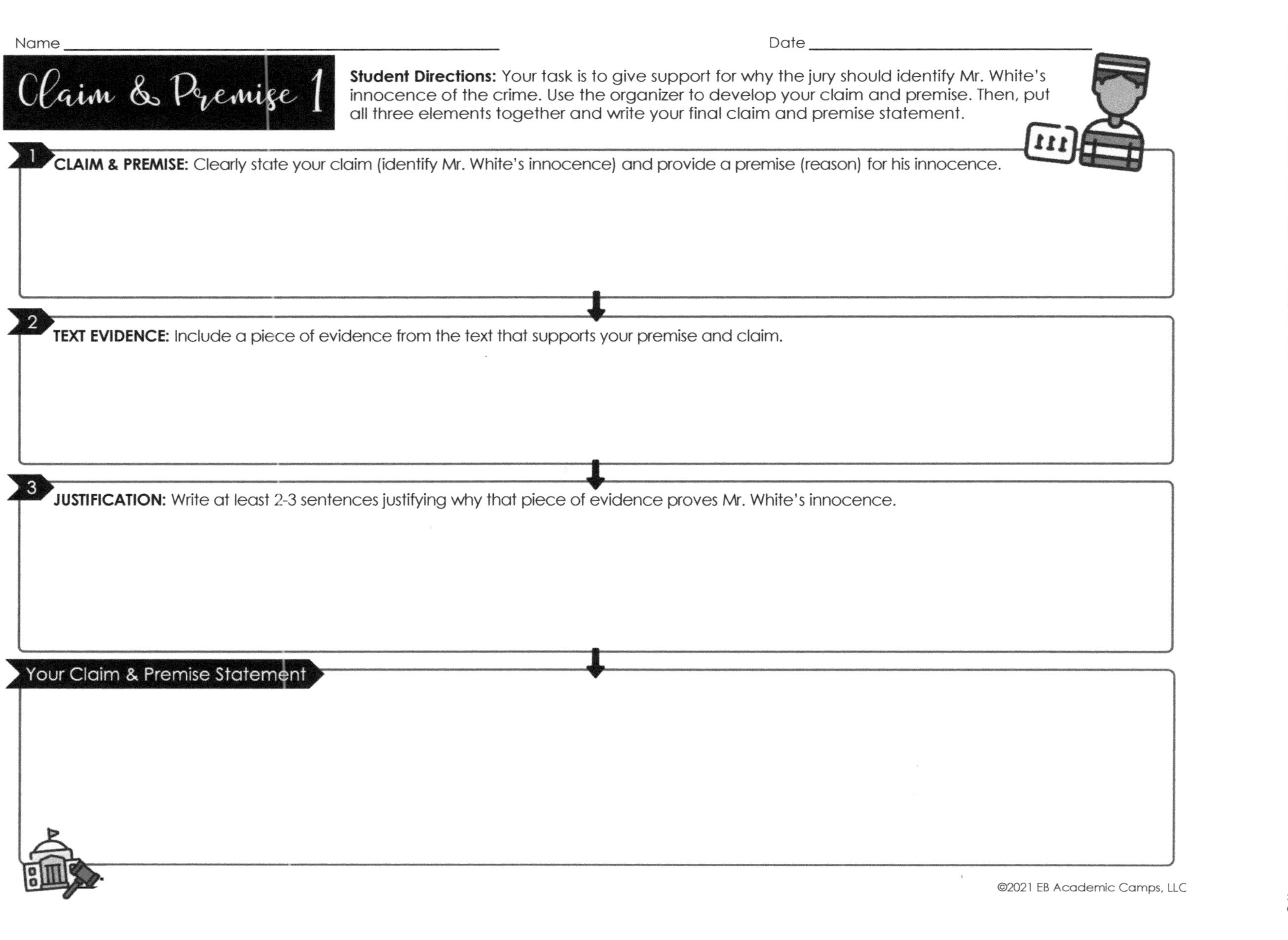

Name ______________________ Date ______________________

Claim & Premise 1

Student Directions: Your task is to give support for why the jury should identify Mr. White's innocence of the crime. Use the organizer to develop your claim and premise. Then, put all three elements together and write your final claim and premise statement.

1 **CLAIM & PREMISE:** Clearly state your claim (identify Mr. White's innocence) and provide a premise (reason) for his innocence.

2 **TEXT EVIDENCE:** Include a piece of evidence from the text that supports your premise and claim.

3 **JUSTIFICATION:** Write at least 2-3 sentences justifying why that piece of evidence proves Mr. White's innocence.

Your Claim & Premise Statement

Name ______________________ Date ______________________

Claim & Premise 2

Student Directions: Your task is to give additional support for why the jury should identify Mr. White's innocence of the crime. Use the organizer to develop your claim and premise. Then, put all three elements together and write your final claim and premise statement.

1 **CLAIM & PREMISE:** Clearly state your claim (identify Mr. White's innocence) and provide a *different* premise (reason) for his innocence.

2 **TEXT EVIDENCE:** Include a *different* piece of evidence from the text that supports your premise and claim.

3 **JUSTIFICATION:** Write at least 2-3 sentences justifying why that piece of evidence proves Mr. White's innocence.

Your Claim & Premise Statement

Name ______________________ Date ______________________

Rebuttal 1

Student Directions: Identify a counter-argument that the prosecution might share. Then rebut, or prove, that the argument is false. Be sure to cite evidence from the text as well as justification. Then, put all three elements together and write your final rebuttal.

1 **COUNTER-ARGUMENT:** Think like the prosecution! Identify an argument they are likely to make in order to prove Mr. White's involvement in the crime.

2 **TEXT EVIDENCE:** Include a piece of evidence from the text that proves why the argument above is false.

3 **JUSTIFICATION:** Write at least 2-3 sentences justifying why that piece of evidence will not hold up in court.

Your Rebuttal Statement

Name ______________________ Date ______________________

Rebuttal 2

Student Directions: Identify a *different* counter-argument that the prosecution might share. Then rebut, or prove, that the argument is false. Be sure to cite evidence from the text as well as justification. Then, put all three elements together and write your final rebuttal.

1 **COUNTER-ARGUMENT:** Think like the prosecution! Identify a *different* argument they are likely to make in order to prove Mr. White's involvement in the crime.

2 **TEXT EVIDENCE:** Include a piece of evidence from the text that proves why the argument above is false.

3 **JUSTIFICATION:** Write at least 2-3 sentences justifying why that piece of evidence will not hold up in court.

Your Rebuttal Statement

Name ________________________ Date ________________________

Closing Statement

Student Directions: Your task is to review, or summarize, the evidence presented during the trial and what each piece of evidence proves or doesn't prove. Use the organizer to outline this information. Then, create your final closing statement. You may use this time to POLITELY discredit the opposing argument. You may also use an emotional appeal if you feel like it will help your case. Ultimately, tell the jury that you want them to find Mr. White innocent of his son's death. Read the example closing statement for inspiration.

Evidence

List specific evidence brought up in the trial here.

Explanation

Give an explanation of what the specific evidence proves or doesn't prove.

Example of a Closing Statement

I want to thank the jury for your time and careful attention during this trial. You've heard all the evidence. You know that Martha Washington is anything but a criminal. The prosecution has put together an interesting case against my client, but their timeline does not add up. Ms. Washington was an exemplary employee who worked for Mr. Gaines for way less money than she should have, but never complained. It is unfortunate that the only time off work she has taken in six years, to care for her mother, gave Mr. Gaines an opportunity to frame her. I know that some of you here are mothers and daughters and employees who give your all. We can all sympathize with Ms. Washington at some level. Let's show her that we hear her and find her innocent of these alleged crimes. Thank you.

Your Closing Statement

Name ______________________ Date ______________________

Opening Statement

Student Directions: Your task is to give an overview of the case to the jury. You can use quotes from the story and allude to some of the evidence your team will be sharing, but you do not want to give everything away! You should only be presenting the facts! Read the tips and tricks below and jot down notes to include in your opening statement. Read the example opening statement for inspiration.

Capture!

Capture the audience's attention by immediately presenting the theme of the case.

Tell!

Tell a story. Using metaphors and descriptive language can help enhance the story and engage jurors.

Connect!

Make a connection with the jury! Don't simply read your opening statement.

Conclude!

End your opening statement by telling the jury the action you would like them to take at the end of the trial. Ask them to rule in your favor!

Example of an Opening Statement

This is a case about a woman who has stolen millions of dollars from my client, Bill Gaines. Mr. Gaines employed her and treated her like family for over six years. Mr. Gaines entrusted her with highly private knowledge of his business and allowed her to handle his bank accounts, both business and personal. She was fired from her position six months ago when she stopped coming to work and proving herself reliable. It was then discovered that she had embezzled money for close to two years. That is why we are here today, ladies and gentlemen of the jury. My name is Ariel Hughes and I represent Mr. Bill Gaines. In this trial, we ask you find the defendant, Martha Washington, guilty of all charges.

Your Opening Statement

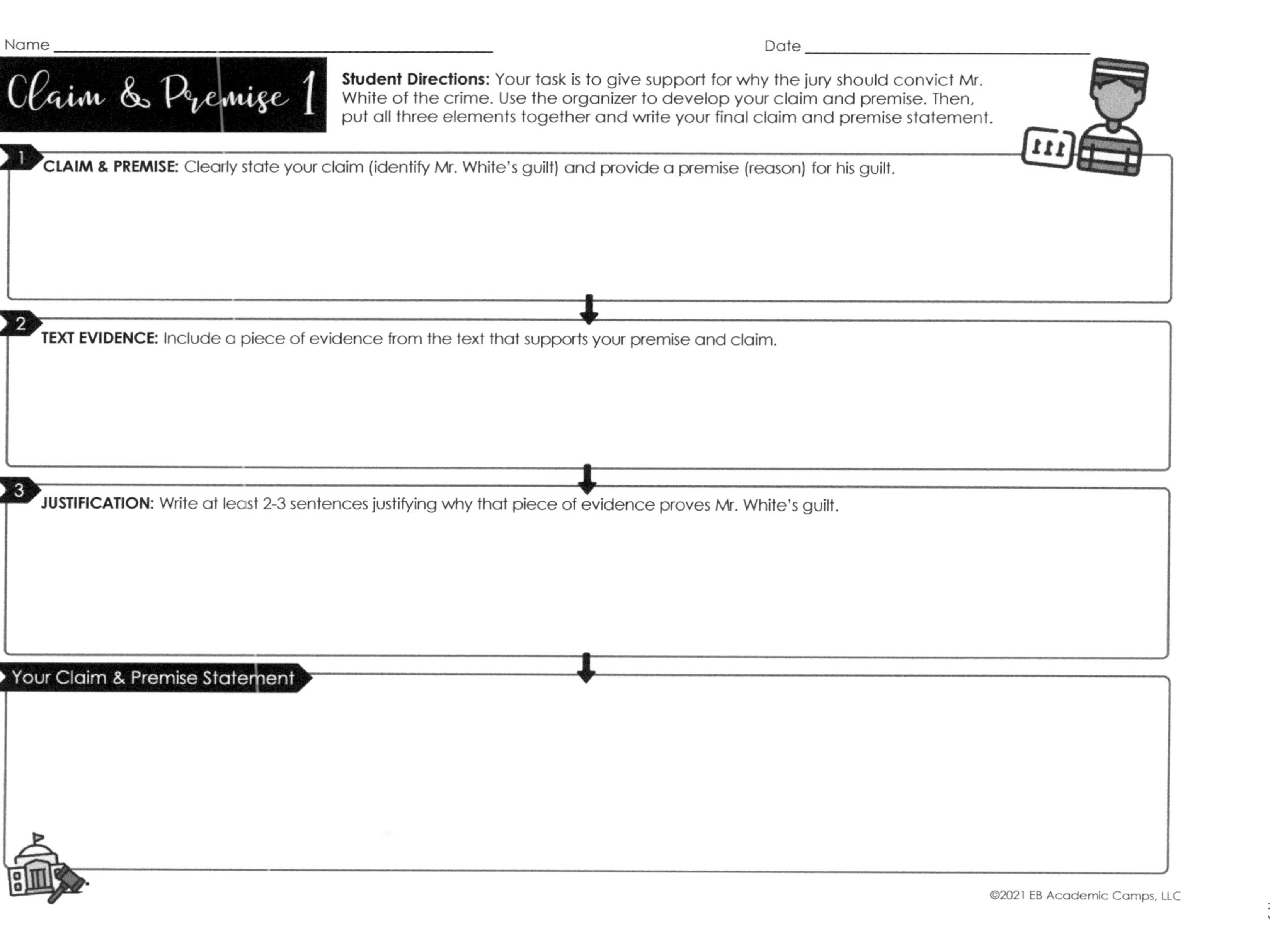

Name ____________________ Date ____________________

Claim & Premise 1

Student Directions: Your task is to give support for why the jury should convict Mr. White of the crime. Use the organizer to develop your claim and premise. Then, put all three elements together and write your final claim and premise statement.

1 **CLAIM & PREMISE:** Clearly state your claim (identify Mr. White's guilt) and provide a premise (reason) for his guilt.

2 **TEXT EVIDENCE:** Include a piece of evidence from the text that supports your premise and claim.

3 **JUSTIFICATION:** Write at least 2-3 sentences justifying why that piece of evidence proves Mr. White's guilt.

Your Claim & Premise Statement

Name ______________________ Date ______________________

Claim & Premise 2

Student Directions: Your task is to give additional support for why the jury should convict Mr. White of the crime. Use the organizer to develop your claim and premise. Then, put all three elements together and write your final claim and premise statement.

1 **CLAIM & PREMISE:** Clearly state your claim (identify Mr. White's guilt) and provide a *different* premise (reason) for his guilt.

2 **TEXT EVIDENCE:** Include a *different* piece of evidence from the text that supports your premise and claim.

3 **JUSTIFICATION:** Write at least 2-3 sentences justifying why that piece of evidence proves Mr. White's guilt.

Your Claim & Premise Statement

Name ______________________ Date ______________________

Rebuttal 1

Student Directions: Identify a counter-argument that the defense might share. (Perhaps a different character's guilt? Something else?) Then rebut, or prove, that the argument is false. Be sure to cite evidence from the text as well as justification. Then, put all three elements together and write your final rebuttal.

1 **COUNTER-ARGUMENT:** Think like the defense! Identify an argument they are likely to make to defend Mr. White.

2 **TEXT EVIDENCE:** Include a piece of evidence from the text that proves why the argument above is false.

3 **JUSTIFICATION:** Write at least 2-3 sentences justifying why that piece of evidence will not hold up in court.

Your Rebuttal Statement

Name ______________________ Date ______________________

Rebuttal 2

Student Directions: Identify a *different* counter-argument that the defense might share. (Perhaps a different character's guilt? Something else?) Then rebut, or prove, that the argument is false. Be sure to cite evidence from the text as well as justification. Then, put all three elements together and write your final rebuttal.

1 **COUNTER-ARGUMENT:** Think like the defense! Identify a *different* argument they are likely to make to defend Mr. White.

2 **TEXT EVIDENCE:** Include a piece of evidence from the text that proves why the argument above is false.

3 **JUSTIFICATION:** Write at least 2-3 sentences justifying why that piece of evidence will not hold up in court.

Your Rebuttal Statement

Name ______________________ Date ______________________

Closing Statement

Student Directions: Your task is to review, or summarize, the evidence presented during the trial and what each piece of evidence proves or doesn't prove. Use the organizer to outline this information. Then, create your final closing statement. You may use this time to POLITELY discredit the opposing argument. You may also use an emotional appeal if you feel like it will help your case. Ultimately, tell the jury that you want them to find Mr. White guilty of his son's death. Read the example closing statement for inspiration.

Evidence

List specific evidence brought up in the trial here.

Explanation

Give an explanation of what the specific evidence proves or doesn't prove.

Example of a Closing Statement

Members of the jury, you have now heard both sides of this case. You know that Mr. Gaines took Ms. Washington in and gave her a job, trusting her to be an integral part of his business. He paid her well and treated her well, as both an employee and a friend. The facts prove that Ms. Washington took advantage of Mr. Gaines and his kindness by stealing from his company. He has suffered not only monetarily from this loss, but also personally. Ms. Washington took from Mr. Gaines the ability to trust in humankind. The defense's argument that Ms. Washington was unaware of the movement of funds is untrue. She is aware of her actions and needs to be punished for her crimes. Thank you for your time and your guilty verdict in this matter.

Your Closing Statement

Name ____________________

Preference Sheet

Student Directions: Read the descriptions for each role in a trial. Indicate your top three choices for participation in the mock trial.

- **PROSECUTION TEAM:** Prove the defendant (Mr. White) is guilty of his son's death.
- **DEFENSE TEAM:** Prove the defendant (Mr. White) is NOT guilty of his son's death.
  - ➢ **OPENING STATEMENT:** Give an overview of the case to the jury from either the defense or the prosecution's perspective.
  - ➢ **CLAIMS:** Identify the facts, from either the defense or the prosecution's perspective, and give specific evidence to support.
  - ➢ **REBUTTALS:** Identify counter-claims, from either the defense or the prosecution's perspective, and give specific evidence to support.
  - ➢ **CLOSING STATEMENT:** Give a summary of the case to the jury from either the defense or the prosecution's perspective.
- **JURY:** Listen to all evidence on both sides of the case (prosecution and defense). Deliberate and make a decision about whether the defendant is guilty or innocent.

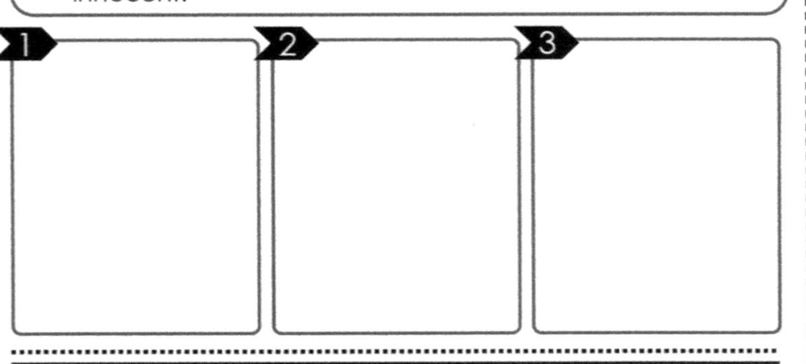

Name ____________________

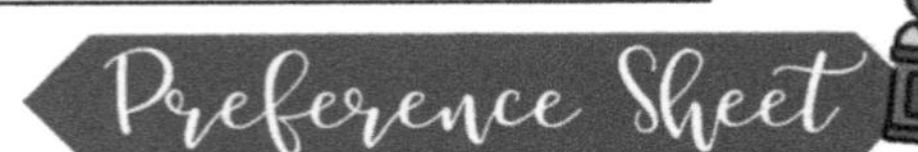

Preference Sheet

Student Directions: Read the descriptions for each role in a trial. Indicate your top three choices for participation in the mock trial.

- **PROSECUTION TEAM:** Prove the defendant (Mr. White) is guilty of his son's death.
- **DEFENSE TEAM:** Prove the defendant (Mr. White is NOT guilty of his son's death.
  - ➢ **OPENING STATEMENT:** Give an overview of the case to the jury from either the defense or the prosecution's perspective.
  - ➢ **CLAIMS:** Identify the facts, from either the defense or the prosecution's perspective, and give specific evidence to support.
  - ➢ **REBUTTALS:** Identify counter-claims, from either the defense or the prosecution's perspective, and give specific evidence to support.
  - ➢ **CLOSING STATEMENT:** Give a summary of the case to the jury from either the defense or the prosecution's perspective.
- **JURY:** Listen to all evidence on both sides of the case (prosecution and defense). Deliberate and make a decision about whether the defendant is guilty or innocent.

1 | 2 | 3

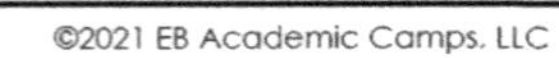

ROMEO AND JULIET MUSIC VIDEO PROJECT

Instructions for Use

The purpose of composing this music video is to help students review, understand, and decipher the text of William Shakespeare's *Romeo and Juliet* in a fun, intriguing, and engaging way.

Students are asked to form a group of 4-5. I allow students to choose their own groups since much of this project will be completed outside of school and forming their own groups makes it a bit easier for them to meet with each other. However, you can absolutely place students into predetermined groups.

I allow students about 75-90 minutes of class time, TOTAL over a few days, to work on this project. I like to give them this time over the first few days when I introduce the project to them because they inevitably have questions upfront. All of the other work is done outside of the classroom. Feel free to allow them as much class time as you would like though!

Directions for Teacher:

1. In their groups, students must first come up with a few songs (so students have some options if they get stuck when they begin writing their lyrics) that they are going to use as their instrumental background music.
2. The teacher *must* first approve these songs before students can even begin writing lyrics for their video. **I highly suggest you look up the lyrics online and use your professional judgment to determine if the song's original lyrics are appropriate for school**. **Even though those lyrics are not being used, the instrumental music still is and alludes to the use of inappropriate language and/or content at school**. The lyrics that students are to compose must either cover the entirety of the novel *OR* cover the entirety of one of the five acts. *(I give students an entire class period – 50 minutes – to work on this portion of the project.)*
3. Once the teacher has approved the songs, students must then generate a concept for their video. I permit students to take complete control over this part of the project to allow for more creativity on their part. Some students have simply done a modern day take on *Romeo and Juliet*, while others have decided to create costumes and settings that reflect ancient Verona or even Elizabethan theatre. I like leaving this open so I can see what they create!
4. I then must approve their lyrics or provide them feedback on their content before they begin filming. I check for the validity of their summaries, their ability to cover the whole play or specific act, creativity, rhyme scheme, figurative language, and originality. Once I have given the "okay," students can now film their videos.
5. Following this step, students are on their own to create original videos. Their only guidelines are outlined in the student handout and the rubric that they are given beforehand.
6. The finished products are almost always incredible, entertaining, engaging, and a great, creative way to finish our *Romeo and Juliet* unit! I hope you and your students enjoy it as much as we do!

Name: ______________________ Date: ______________________

Romeo and Juliet

MUSIC VIDEO PROJECT

For this project you will be creating and filming your own music video! Please follow the outlined directions below to ensure a good grade and a positive learning experience.

Directions:

1. Choose **4-5 classmates** to create a group for this project. Write their names, phone numbers, and email addresses here:

- ______________________
- ______________________
- ______________________
- ______________________
- ______________________

2. Decide on **2-3 songs** you might like to use for your video. *(Note: These songs must be school appropriate and approved by me before you can move forward.)*

- ______________________
- ______________________
- ______________________

3. Create a **CONCEPT**. Meaning, are you going to do a modern day take on *Romeo and Juliet*, or create costumes and settings that reflect ancient Verona or even Elizabethan theatre? I am going to leave this up to you and your creativity, but I do need to see the concept before you can move forward.

4. Begin **WRITING** the lyrics to your song. Your song must cover the span of the entirety of the play OR the entirety of one of the acts from the play. Whatever you choose, make sure to include elements of rhyme, figurative language, and understanding and comprehension of the text and main message(s) or theme(s) of the play. *(Note: Before you can begin filming your video, it is highly suggested that you get your lyrics approved by me.)*

5. Start **FILMING** your music video! Please make sure to carefully review the rubrics so you know how you will be graded and what is expected for "A" work versus "C" work. Good luck and have fun with this!

FINAL DUE DATE: ______________________

FIVE-WORD WONDER

✓ PREP

Choose five unique but important words and/or phrases from the text you will be reading. For example, if you were reading "Thank You, M'am" by Langston Hughes, you might choose: "Thank you, M'am, Mrs. Luella Bates Washington Jones, run, boy, and blue suede shoes."

✓ DAY OF LESSON

Without telling students what text they will be reading, write the five words and/or phrases on the board. Arrange students into groups of 3-4. Explain to them that they will be writing their own anticipatory paragraph explaining what they believe the story will be about. The only hints they have are the words/phrases you have listed.

Allow each group about ten minutes to predict what the text is about and write their anticipatory paragraph. Students must include the words/phrases in their writing. Each group should share their paragraphs aloud.

Optional: Before students write their paragraphs, tell them some awards are up for grabs! You will be awarding groups special ribbons based on what they write. The awards can include: Most Accurate, Couldn't Be Further From the Truth, Most Humorous, Most Creative, and Publish Worthy. After students have read the text, distribute the awards to each group based on who you feel deserves each one. (Displaying students' paragraphs along with the awards makes for a great bulletin board display!)

Name: ____________________ Date: ____________________

FIVE-WORD WONDER

paragraph

Students Directions: Using the five words you were provided, predict what the text is about by writing an anticipatory paragraph. You must include the words/phrases you were given in your writing. Be prepared to share your paragraph aloud.

five words

anticipatory paragraph

INDEX

ABOUT THE AUTHORS

CAITLIN MITCHELL AND JESSICA CANNATA are middle school ELA teachers and the founders of EB Academics, an organization on a mission to provide teachers with engaging and rigorous ELA lessons. Both Mitchell and Cannata have master's degrees with focuses in curriculum development and secondary education, and they both have been named Outstanding Teachers of the Year by the LAX Coastal Chamber of Commerce. They founded EB Academics with the desire to help English teachers find success in their reading and writing curriculum while offering a community of like-minded educators. Through their online EB Writing Program and monthly membership, the EB Teachers' Club, they have helped thousands of middle school ELA teachers support their students in mastering standards.

CPSIA information can be obtained
at www.ICGtesting.com
Printed in the USA
BVHW020817040621
608816BV00011B/185